The 10
Cornerstones of Selling

The Avant® Professional Sales Series

The 10
Cornerstones of Selling

How to Get Greater
Control of Your Selling Results

Andoni Lizardy

Avant Books®
San Marcos, California

Library of Congress Cataloging-in-Publication Data

Lizardy, Andoni
The 10 conerstones of selling:
how to get greater control of your selling results
Glossary
Includes index
1. Selling   2. Selling—Problems, exercises, etc.
I. Title   II. Title: Ten cornerstones of selling   III. Series
HF5438.25.L588   1992
658.8'5—dc20   LCCN 91-70004

ISBN 0-932238-62-9

Avant Books®
Slawson Communications, Inc.
San Marcos, California 92069-1436

Printed in the United States

Interior design by Teena Eber
Cover design by Ed Roxburgh
Cover photograph by Jim Santini

This book is dedicated to my friends and associates Richard Burin and Regina Zekis. Their exceptional training efforts have helped thousands of people become more effective and more professional.

This book is also dedicated to the men and women who have trusted their employees to the care and guidance of Lizardy Associates. Thank you for your confidence.

My Special Thanks...

to Kathleen Webber, Teena Eber, Rita Hoepp and Linnea Dayton, who have spent countless hours in reviewing, critiquing and editing this series of books. For all your efforts, encouragement and patience I am extremely grateful.

Contents

1 . . . . *1*

The 10 Cornerstones

Identifying the Cornerstones of Selling
  1. Presenting Features, Advantages and Benefits
  2. Using the WIIFM Technique
  3. Recognizing Buying Signals
  4. Asking the Right Questions
  5. Handling Objections
  6. Placing the Customer in the Picture of Success
  7. Pairing
  8. Romancing the Sale
  9. Stressing the Difference
  10. Using Transitional Phrases
Chapter Summary

2 . . . . *13*

Talking About What Interests the Customer

Presenting Features, Advantages and Benefits
Using the WIIFM Technique
Recognizing Buying Signals
Chapter Summary

Tables

About the Author

Andoni Lizardy, president of Lizardy Associates, is a management consultant, speaker and author of twelve business books and courses dealing with sales, sales management, sales planning, negotiations, customer relations, communications, business psychology and time management. He is also a salesperson who sells products and services both nationally and internationally.

He has trained tens of thousands of sales, marketing, and customer service people as well as sales and general managers. Since developing courses for the world's largest management association, over half of the top Fortune 500 Companies have sent people to his seminars—while a number of American, Asian and European companies employee him as a consultant.

As a much sought after keynote speaker, he lectures internationally in London, Zurich, Athens, Cairo, Singapore, Hong Kong, Tokyo, Edmonton, and Toronto, for a wide variety of associations and business organizations.

Andoni Lizardy has also lectured at Kent State University and has guest lectured at the University of Toronto, University of Pittsburgh and the University of Pennsylvania's Wharton School of Business. He divides his consulting and speaking time between North America, Asia, Europe, and the Far East.

Introduction

For those interested
in the subtle nuances of selling
that make excellent salespeople successful.

This book examines skills salespeople ofter overlook, skills that must be mastered well if they expect to sell successfully. In this book you will discover:

- Who initiates buying signals.

- What pairing is and how to use it.

- When and how to romance the sale.

- Why the WIIFM technique is critical to your success.

- Where common selling mistakes occur and how to avoid them.

Plus how to:

- Use transitional phrases.

- Ask questions more effectively.

- Place the customer in the picture of success.

- Handle customer objections more professionally.

- Stress the difference between you and your competition.

- Use features, advantages and benefits to your advantage.

My staff and I have conducted seminars for tens of thousands of salespeople, customer contact people, and their managers all over the world. These experiences have led us to realize that most selling challenges, needs and shortcomings are similar regardless of culture, product or service. These experiences have also led me to realize that sales and other customer contact people make their greatest selling errors as a result of not using the cornerstones effectively.

For these reasons this book is a valuable tool for those of you who sincerely want to learn how to sell better. This small book offers you a large amount of information. If you skim read, picking up a few ideas here and there—you will extend the time it takes for you to develop your selling skills.

A special *thank you* for your interest in this book, and may you master the Cornerstones of Selling.

Best wishes,

ANDONI LIZARDY

1

The 10 Cornerstones

*Every step and element of the sale
is dependent upon the 10 cornerstones
of selling. Those who learn these practices
succeed as communicators and as salespeople.*

One of my friends is an extremely successful salesperson who became successful by turning negative situations into positive opportunities. This skill has served her well. Her first sales position was with a company in Chicago. Her persuasive communication skills and winning ways convinced her sales manager that she was the right person for a challenging role. So, they sent her to sell in Detroit.

Her top prospects were General Motors, Ford, and Chrysler. In those days the Detroit market was male-dominated, so sexism was an issue with which she would have to contend. Typically, male-oriented businesses deal only with other males. Her manager did not prepare or warn her of this challenge.

Being Eurasian, racism was another issue she would have to overcome. Most of the buyers were white and preferred dealing with white vendors. Her manager did not prepare or warn her of this challenge either. She was one of the first nonwhites to sell in a white-dominated market.

However, the greatest challenge of all was her company's track record of insensitivity to its customers. The company had once enjoyed the business of the automobile industry, but had angered them by closing the local office. They discovered that they were without local service and product support only when they dialed the vendor's Detroit number and received a tape-recorded message referring them to a Chicago number. Again, her manager did not warn her.

Within twenty-four months she overcame these hurdles and won back three of the four largest prospects in her territory. She became one of the company's top salespeople and money earners. Those who listen and observe the way she sells understand why she is so successful. Her greatest strengths are a positive manner, persistence in the face of adversity, and an ability to *read* people and respond in an appropriate fashion. Finally, of all the salespeople I have ever met, she possesses the greatest skill in using the 10 cornerstones of selling (also known as the subelements of the sale).

Unlike many of her peers, this lady understands that selling success is due to a variety of factors. One factor essential to her selling effectiveness is the use of the cornerstones. She recognizes that her presentation and closing efforts are dependent upon these subelements and skillfully employs them as needed.

This book suggests ways to use these cornerstones. Once mastered, they will help the readers become more effective communicators and more successful salespeople.

Identifying the Cornerstones of Selling

The subelements of the sale are critical to the selling process. They are so vital to the selling process that this book refers to them as the *Cornerstones of Selling* because:

- They are practices that support The Five Steps of the Sale (see *Table 1-1*). Without the subelements the five steps cannot be effectively executed.
- They are practices that support the seller. Few salespeople ever become consistently successful without mastering these techniques.
- The cornerstones are communication tools that salespeople can use to:
  - Further explain their positions.
  - Capitalize on important points.
  - Better address their prospects' responses.
- Like the cornerstone of a building, the cornerstones of selling support the entire sales communications process for both buyers and sellers.

The cornerstones (or subelements) of selling include:

1. Presenting features, advantages and benefits.
2. Using the WIIFM technique.
3. Recognizing buying signals.
4. Asking the right questions.
5. Handling objections.
6. Placing the customer in the picture of success.
7. Pairing.
8. Romancing the sale.
9. Stressing the difference.
10. Using transitional phrases.

Each of these subelements can be found in at least one place within the five steps of the sale. *The Anatomy of the Sale, Table 1-1,* summarizes the five steps outlined in the *Avant Professional Sales Series* book *1st Impressions.* In addition, throughout this book tables appear, such as the one that follows, each designed to help the reader better visualize how to use a given sales technique.

The Anatomy of the Sale
Table 1-1
Summary of the Five Steps of the Sale; Each Step's Purposes and Practices

Purpose of Each Step	Practice— Salesperson's Role
Step 1—Greeting	
1. Allows the seller to introduce self to the buyer	1. Smile and offer the prospect a positive greeting.
2. Allows the prospect to introduce self to the seller.	2. Offer a firm handshake (if culture permits).
3. Allows prospect and seller to exchange business cards.	3. Offer a business card and request a card from the buyer.
Step 2—Warm-up	
1. Gives the prospect time to relax and get comfortable	1. Talk about the prospect's interests or organization.
2. Gives the seller time to adjust to the environment and compose himself or herself	2. Breathe deeply, think in positive terms and smile.
3. Both are given the opportunity to begin evaluating each other's personality, values, likes and dislikes.	3. Use common sense and understanding of people to evaluate the prospect's personality, values, likes and dislikes.

Continued on next page.

Continued from previous page.

Step 3—Qualification

1. Allows the seller to decide if the prospect is a legitimate buyer or merely a shopper.

2. Allows the prospect to observe and listen to the seller and evaluate the seller as a possible vendor.

3. Allows seller to search for possible buyer sales resistance (fear or dislike of the seller, the vendor, the company, service or product).

1. Thoroughly evaluate the situation and the prospect's needs by asking the Six W's (see *Glossary*).

2. Behave professionally— asking logical questions, listening, and responding responsibly.

3. Ask the prospect about his or her knowledge of (or previous experience with) the service, product or vendor's organization.

Step 4—Presentation

1. Based upon the previous steps, this one allows the seller to give the prospect enough data to make a buying decision.

2. Leads both prospect and seller to the close in a natural, positive and collaborative fashion.

1. Make a personalized presentation that appeals to the buyer's needs, desires, behavior, values and interests.

2. Use features, advantages and benefits that appeal to the prospect and lead to an agreement (the close).

Step 5—Close

1. Allows the buyer and the seller to agree to:
- Set an appointment.
- Place seller on vendor list.
- Allow seller to gather data.
- Place an order or trial order.
- Set buying and selling terms.
- Pay monies owed the vendor.
- Meet with the decision maker.
- A presentation or demonstration.
- Meet with the buying committee.

1. Seek agreement with the prospect by using:
- A variety of trial closes.
- A courteous, positive and persistent attitude.
- Closes that appeal to the prospect's personality.
- The best and strongest close in later closing stages.
- The prospect's ideas and phrases to answer his or her questions or objections.

Anticipating and Preparing To Meet the Customer's Expectations

The successful execution of the five steps of the sale are dependent upon the seller understanding how to:

- Use the cornerstones of the sale.
- React to prospect questions, objections and comments.

Preparing for all eventualities is a challenging exercise. With time and experience the salesperson will know how to answer questions accurately, such as:

- What is my unique selling proposition?
- Why should the prospect buy from me?
- What can I do to serve my customer better?
- Am I dressed in an appropriate and professional fashion?
- Are my proposals more (or less) effective than my competition's?
- What is my strategy for succeeding in sales? What are my tactics?
- Are my presentations more (or less) effective than my competition's?
- Should I use a form outlining my key questions when calling on prospects?
- Do my briefcase, calling cards, and supporting materials promote a positive and professional image?
- How can I show my prospects the differences between my organization and the competition without appearing unfair, petty or negative?
- Regarding my samples, proposals, leave-behinds, and other selling props:
  - Are they effective?
  - Why am I using them?
  - Am I using them well?
  - Do they help clarify my message?
  - Am I comfortable when I use them?
  - Should they be updated or upgraded?
  - Do they impress my prospects favorably?
  - Are they helping me to sell my products and services?

- Personally speaking:
  - Do I really care about my profession?
  - Do I really care about helping my prospects?
  - Am I committed to my organization's success?
  - Am I willing to sacrifice a short-term gain for long-term success?
  - Am I committed to a well-defined and high level of selling excellence?
  - Do I know enough about selling and negotiating to make professional and positive impressions on others?
  - Do I know enough about my products, my services, my organization, the competition and my prospects to make a credible impression on my prospect?
  - Am I keeping current in market changes that may affect my company, prospects, and customers? Do I understand the product and service upgrades, new sales and communications techniques, and legal, social and environmental factors?

These issues affect the way salespeople deal with their prospects and customers. The resulting attitudes can be so strong that they affect the way sellers use (or avoid using) the cornerstones of selling.

The Importance of Understanding the Cornerstones

One of our clients once asked me to review a sales flip chart presentation that his company had just purchased. It was an unusual meeting that began in the chief executive officer's (CEO) office. Gathered around his desk were the CEO, the president of the organization, one of my staff members and me.

"Please look at the new sales presentation a company put together for our staff. It cost us about $26,000 and we would like your opinion as our sales and marketing consultant," the CEO stated with a smile.

"Yes," smiled the president. "The flip chart is good. We're going to use it in tomorrow's national sales meeting. I'm going to introduce it myself. Perhaps you could support my presentation when you address the group. Review it and give us your opinion."

My silence must have bothered the president, as he insisted, "Relax, sit back and enjoy the presentation."

He pulled a large three-color flip chart from what appeared to be an expensive, custom-cut, oversized case and began his presentation. His talk was long and boring. Finally he finished.

The CEO was eager to hear my opinion. The president, confident of my analysis, encouraged me to speak by asking, "Well, what do you think?"

My first few words came out rapidly. "It's a beautiful flip chart and you have a nice carrying case for it. The colors are appealing." Then I hesitated.

Everyone smiled.

"Go on," the president urged. "What do you think about it? I mean the whole thing."

"It does everything—except one thing," I stated in a low tone.

"What's that?" asked the CEO.

"It doesn't sell your products," I added.

Both men immediately became upset. The president leaned over the CEO's desk and pushed the intercom button. He then ordered his secretary to call the vice president of sales and the vice president of marketing into his office immediately.

"Now before we go into my office," the president demanded, "show me what's wrong with this chart!"

"Too large," I answered. "Ever see salespeople carry charts that large to their customers' offices? These charts will spend the first three months in the back seats of your sellers' cars. Then they'll spend the next three months in car trunks. From there your salespeople will move them to their hall closets. Three years from now they will pull them out, dust them off, look at them, laugh, and then throw them away. They're just too large."

"But we spent a fortune on the carrying cases," insisted the CEO.

Incredible, I thought. *His concern is with the carrying case rather than the effectiveness of his salespeople's presentations.*

"Too large," I replied.

The president snapped, "Okay, let's do what we must to make this thing work."

"Make any changes necessary," demanded the CEO. "But don't change the size of those flip charts. I spent a fortune on those cases!"

"Where do we start?" asked the president.

"Let's look at what else is wrong with the chart," I suggested in a gentle tone.

"Good," the president said. "Begin."

"The presentation is too long and too technical. You are selling at the customer—and nobody wants to be sold at. The written copy doesn't (*a*) stress customer benefits, (*b*) anticipate and answer common customer objections, or (*c*) call for a positive conclusion by the customer. It isn't written with the prospect in mind."

Stories like this are common. Every day thousands of sellers fail to represent themselves well because they do not understand the cornerstones of selling. Understanding and using the cornerstones effectively is critical because the cornerstones:

- Are selling tools.
- Curry the prospect's favor.
- Help salespeople win prospect confidence.
- Help sellers appear and sound more professional.
- Make the sale a positive experience for the prospect.
- Assist sellers in making more effective sales presentations.
- Offer salespeople ways to focus attention on important issues.
- Present salespeople with ways to personalize the selling process.
- Are essential to the successful implementation of the five selling steps.
- Aid sellers in guiding their prospects to and through the closing process.
- Give salespeople techniques that they can use to communicate with their prospects.
- Support sellers in moving from one step of the sale to another smoothly and with continuity.
- Guide salespeople in their efforts to handle prospect objections.
- Help turn prospect objections into selling opportunities.

Chapter Summary

1. The cornerstones of selling are also the subelements of a sale.
2. The five steps of the sale are:
   - Greeting
   - Warm-up
   - Qualification
   - Presentation
   - Close
3. The subelements include:
   - Presenting features, advantages and benefits.
   - Using the WIIFM technique.
   - Recognizing buying signals.
   - Asking the right questions.
   - Handling objections.
   - Placing the customer in the picture of success.
   - Pairing.
   - Romancing the sale.
   - Stressing the difference.
   - Using transitional phrases.
4. Your understanding and effective use of the cornerstones is critical because the cornerstones:
   - Are selling tools.
   - Curry the prospect's favor.
   - Help you to win prospect confidence.
   - Help you appear and sound more professional.
   - Offer you ways to focus attention on important issues.
   - Make the sale a positive experience for your prospects.
   - Aid you in making more effective sales presentations.
   - Present you with ways to personalize the selling process.
   - Are essential to your successfully implementing the five selling steps.

- Aid you in guiding your prospects to and through the closing process.
- Give you techniques that you can use to communicate with your prospects.
- Support you in moving from one step of the sale to another smoothly and with continuity.
- Guide you in your efforts to handle objections from your prospect.
- Help you turn prospect objections into selling opportunities.

2

Talking About What Interests the Customer

*Everyone is the center
of his or her universe.*

One day a friend of mine, who has over a decade's experience as a professional purchasing agent, began complaining to me about salespeople.

"I'm so tired of talking to salespeople," she said. "It's difficult trying to communicate with people who just don't listen."

"Having problems with your vendors?" I asked politely.

"Yes. Let me give you an example," she responded. "Just a few minutes before you arrived one of the salespeople from a vendor was here. During his sales call I told him exactly what I wanted. Instead of verifying what I wanted, he kept switching the topic to what *he wanted* to sell me. Clearly I wasn't interested in what he was presenting, but he persisted."

"Is he normally a poor listener?"

"No. For nearly a year he has called on us. He is usually a good listener and responds well to my questions and needs. In other words, he's normally an excellent salesperson and a pleasure to work with. But this time he just wasn't listening to me. Well, I got irritated. When he realized I was upset, he became defensive."

"How did you react to his defensiveness?"

"I became more irritated with him, and he became more defensive. His interest is not in me as a person—he is only interested in making a sale."

"Then what happened?" I asked.

"I told him, for the third time, that I couldn't afford anything more than his least expensive products. My company's cash flow restricts my budget and right now the cash is not flowing."

"Then what happened?"

"Suddenly logic started to take over my thinking process. I calmed myself down and helped him regain his composure as well."

"Do you think he may be suffering from a lack of sales training?"

"No," she answered. "I know the company, its owners and staff very well. They're well-trained and well-compensated. The problem was that he displayed little customer sensitivity. In a more kind and patient moment I pointed that out to him and explained why I became angry. And then I told him what he could have done to recover from the situation."

"So he lost the sale?"

"He had built up a lot of good will through our previous meetings. Therefore, I made a special effort to overlook his behavior. We both apologized for overreacting and I gave him an order."

"Is this kind of incident common?"

"You mean a seller not listening to a buyer's requests and needs?"

"Right."

"It happens too often. I'll bet you I meet a salesperson every day who fails to listen to some vital points I'm trying to make."

"What bothers you most about salespeople who are not meeting your needs?"

"Poor listening habits. Lack of sensitivity, sincerity, and concern for the other person. Refusing to understand the other person's point of view. And a few more."

"Like?"

"The other buyers inside my company and I listed mistakes salespeople make. There must have been fifteen major mistakes, but several kept popping up on each of our lists."

Here are the three mistakes she and her associates claim sellers most often commit:

- Inability to talk in terms that interest the prospect.
- A tendency to oversell features that the prospect does not intend to purchase.
- Failure to show the prospect how the organization, family, or individual will profit from the purchase.

In our story, the seller forgot to employ the winning strategies that made him successful during past sales calls. Among his many errors, the seller had abandoned two important selling practices:

(1) Turning feature statements into customer benefits.

(2) Explaining to prospects how they will profit from the purchase (the WIIFM technique).

While these practices are similar, there are some major differences between the techniques, as described later. This chapter includes presenting features, advantages and benefits, using the WIIFM technique and recognizing buying signals.

Evaluating Your Understanding of the Cornerstones of Selling

Part I—Buying Signals, What's in it for Me, and Features, Advantages and Benefits

The following chapters include a self-assessment exercise for those interested in evaluating their knowledge and usage of the cornerstones of selling. These exercises were developed during a fifteen-year period with over 10,000 salespeople, sales managers, and other customer contact people in:

- Nearly 2,500 actual selling and customer contact situations.
- Over 8,200 roleplay exercises evaluated by myself and the Lizardy Associates' assessment team.

The questions, answers, scoring values, and classifications are based on the performances and attitudes of those who participated.

Exercise Suggestions

In the interest of accuracy please review the following suggestions:

√   Move as rapidly as possible through these exercises, avoid over analyzing any question or answer.

√   If you have difficulty responding objectively to any of the following questions, ask someone experienced and qualified in sales (and who has watched you sell in a variety of situations) to respond to these questions as if he or she were you.

√   Avoid guessing or using the process of deduction to arrive at any answer you do not know. Select only those answers that show the way you actually perform—not the way you think you should sell, or would like to sell. In other words, avoid responding to a statement if your normal practice differs from it.

This exercise and the others found in this book are neither tests nor contests. These studies and the Probable Tendencies tables that follow evaluate your understanding of the cornerstones of selling. Each deals with a specific cornerstone:

Part I.   Buying Signals, What's in it for Me, and Features, Advantages and Benefits

Part II.   Asking Questions and Handling Objections

Part III.   Pairing, Romancing the Sale, and Placing the Customer in the Picture of Success

Part IV.   Transitional Phrases and Stressing the Difference

These reviews are relativity exercises that allow you to select your most common practice from several options. Because of the scoring process, you must limit your selections to one choice for every statement. Each statement and choice realistically reflects actual selling situations and options. All this should help you to understand that your conduct and attitude affect the way you communicate and sell.

Each study gives the opportunity to evaluate which selling style you are most likely to exhibit in relationship to the exercise's topic. Regardless of how well you do, the most important score is reflected in your performance, your sense of selfworth and your customers' willingness to buy your product.

Exercise

Cornerstones of Selling Study
Part I—Buying Signals, What's in it
for Me, and Features, Advantages and Benefits

Instructions:

Check the letter next to the answer that is most accurate. Please mark only one selection for each question. For example:

0.	I like to sell to:
	a. New prospects.
	b. People I know.
√	c. It doesn't matter.

In making your selections:

- Do not mark any phrase you are uncertain of or that does not apply.
- Check the *Glossary* or *Index* for any word that is unfamiliar.
- Be as honest as possible, and mark the way you actually perform or behave.

---

1. A feature is a statement about:
    a. My product, service, terms, staff or organization.
    b. What my product or service will do for the prospect.
    c. How the prospect will profit from my product or service.

2. An advantage is a comment about:
    a. My product, service, terms, staff or organization.
    b. What my product or service will do for the prospect.
    c. How the prospect will profit from my product or service.

3. A benefit is a comment about:
    a. My product, service, terms, staff or organization.
    b. What my product or service will do for the prospect.
    c. How the prospect will profit from my product or service.

---

4. I tend to talk more about:

    a. Features than advantages.

    b. Advantages and benefits than features.

    c. Features than benefits.

5. I can use the following phrases interchangeably:

    a. Features and benefits.

    b. Advantages and features.

    c. Advantages and benefits.

6. When I present features, I:

    a. Offer as many features as possible.

    b. Follow up key features with benefit statements.

    c. Am not certain how I present features.

7. If I convert a product or service feature into a benefit, I:

    a. Do so during the qualification and presentation.

    b. Do so only during the presentation stage.

    c. Do not use this selling technique.

8. Which of the following is a feature statement?

    a. "This boat engine is the largest available anywhere."

    b. "You will enjoy the ease of starting this engine."

    c. "You will save time and money with this engine."

9. Which of the following is an advantage statement?

    a. "This is the most reliable boat engine available."

    b. "This boat engine never fails."

    c. "You will never again worry about engine failure."

10. Which of the following is a benefits statement?

    a. "This is a twin engine boat."

    b. "You will increase your fuel savings by over 10 percent."

    c. "This is the most powerful boat engine available."

11. I try to think (analyze things or view things) like my buyers do:

   a. Yes.

   b. No.

   c. Sometimes.

12. I explain to others how they gain from my product or service:

   a. When it occurs to me to do so.

   b. On a regular basis.

   c. Almost never. My prospects know what they gain.

13. Empathizing with my prospects and customers is something:

   a. I attempt to avoid.

   b. I do when it occurs to me to do so.

   c. I do often.

14. Regarding my prospects' and customers' needs:

   a. I ask regularly and recheck during every sales call.

   b. I am aware, so I rarely recheck them after an initial sales call.

   c. I know them, so I rarely, if ever, ask questions about my customers' needs.

15. I use different techniques to personalize benefits for the prospect:

   a. Never.

   b. Frequently.

   c. Rarely.

16. I point out how buyers gain from my product or service by:

   a. Telling prospects what they will gain.

   b. Showing prospects what they will gain.

   c. Getting prospects to tell me what they will gain.

17. I anticipate what the prospect needs and wants to hear:

   a. During the sales call.

   b. Before and during the sales call.

   c. I rarely anticipate these things since prospects eventually reveal them.

18. My abiliy to explain what prospects gain from my products or services is:

    a. Poor.

    b. Fair.

    c. Excellent.

19. Which statement answers the prospect's question, "What's in it for me?"

    a. "Our installation people are very professional."

    b. "You can use this unit at home and at work."

    c. "This unit is the most highly rated system in the industry."

20. Which statement answers the prospect's question, "What's in it for me?"

    a. "This is a good service and our company is very reliable."

    b. "Our group is the most experienced vendor in the area."

    c. "You'll save money every time you use this service."

21. I know what a buying signal is:

    a. Yes.

    b. No.

    c. I can guess its meaning.

22. I can identify buying signals easily:

    a. Yes.

    b. No.

    c. Sometimes.

23. A buying signal is an indication from the:

    a. Seller that he or she is buying what the prospect is saying.

    b. Prospect that he or she may have a question.

    c. Prospect that he or she may be ready to buy.

24. I consciously listen for buying signals:

    a. Yes.

    b. No.

    c. Sometimes.

25. When I hear a buying signal, I:
    a. Answer with a closing statement or question.
    b. Respond to the signal and then attempt to close.
    c. I don't normally listen for buying signals.
26. "How many sizes are there?" is a buying signal:
    a. Yes.
    b. No.
    c. Possibly.
27. "I'll buy it if my boss agrees" is a buying signal:
    a. Yes.
    b. No.
    c. Possibly.
28. "Do these come in green?" is a buying signal:
    a. Yes.
    b. No.
    c. Possibly.
29. "What if I don't like it once I buy it?" is a buying signal:
    a. Yes.
    b. No.
    c. Usually.
30. "How soon can you deliver it?" is a buying signal:
    a. Yes.
    b. No.
    c. Usually.

Scoring

Cornerstones of Selling Study
Part I—Buying Signals, What's in it
for Me, and Features, Advantages and Benefits

Instructions:

From the previous *Exercise*, circle the same letters below, including the score. After completing this section, proceed to the *Score Box*. Make certain your answers reflect the way you actually interact with your prospects and customers.

Legend:

BYS   — Buying Signals.
WIIFM — What's in It for Me.
FAB   — Features, Advantages and Benefits.

---

1. A feature is a statement about:

    a. 10 FAB

    b. 0

    c. 0

2. An advantage is a comment about:

    a. 0

    b. 10 FAB

    c. 10 FAB

3. A benefit is a comment about:

    a. 0

    b. 10 FAB

    c. 10 FAB

4. I tend to talk more about:

    a. 0

    b. 10 FAB

    c. 0

5. I can use the following phrases interchangeably:
   a. 0
   b. 0
   c. 10 FAB

6. When I present features, I:
   a. 0
   b. 10 FAB
   c. 0

7. If I convert a product or service feature into a benefit, I:
   a. 10 FAB
   b. 5 FAB
   c. 0

8. Which of the following is a feature statement?
   a. 10 FAB
   b. 0
   c. 0

9. Which of the following is an advantage statement?
   a. 0
   b. 0
   c. 10 FAB

10. Which of the following is a benefits statement?
    a. 0
    b. 10 FAB
    c. 0

11. I try to think (analyze things or view things) like my buyers do:
    a. 10 WIIFM
    b. 0
    c. 5 WIIFM

---

12. I explain to others how they gain from my product or service:

    a. 5 WIIFM

    b. 10 WIIFM

    c. 0

13. Empathizing with my prospects and customers is something:

    a. 0

    b. 5 WIIFM

    c. 10 WIIFM

14. Regarding my prospects' and customers' needs, I:

    a. 10 WIIFM

    b. 0

    c. 0

15. I use differing techniques to personalize benefits for the prospect:

    a. 0

    b. 10 WIIFM

    c. 0

16. I point out how buyers gain from my product or service by:

    a. 5 WIIFM

    b. 7 WIIFM

    c. 10 WIIFM

17. I anticipate what the prospect needs and wants to hear:

    a. 5 WIIFM

    b. 10 WIIFM

    c. 0

18. My ability to explain what prospects gain from my products or services is:

    a. 0

    b. 5 WIIFM

    c. 10 WIIFM

19. Which statement answers the prospect's question, "What's in it for me?"

    a. 0

    b. 10 WIIFM

    c. 0

20. Which statement answers the prospect's question, "What's in it for me?"

    a. 0

    b. 0

    c. 10 WIIFM

21. I know what a buying signal is:

    a. 10 BYS

    b. 0

    c. 0

22. I can identify buying signals easily:

    a. 10 BYS

    b. 0

    c. 5 BYS

23. A buying signal is an indication from the:

    a. 0

    b. 0

    c. 10 BYS

24. I consciously listen for buying signals:

    a. 10 BYS

    b. 0

    c. 5 BYS

25. When I hear a buying signal, I:

    a. 5 BYS

    b. 10 BYS

    c. 0

26. "How many sizes are there?" is a buying signal:

 a. 0

 b. 0

 c. 10 BYS

27. "I'll buy it if my boss agrees." is a buying signal:

 a. 10 BYS

 b. 0

 c. 5 BYS

28. "Do these come in green?" is a buying signal:

 a. 5 BYS

 b. 0

 c. 10 BYS

29. "What if I don't like it once I buy it?" is a buying signal:

 a. 10 BYS

 b. 0

 c. 10 BYS

30. "How soon can you deliver it?" is a buying signal:

 a. 10 BYS

 b. 0

 c. 10 BYS

Score Box
Cornerstones of Selling Study
Part I—Buying Signals, What's in it
for Me, and Features, Advantages and Benefits
Instructions:

Total your score for each category and place it on the line to the right of the appropriate classification:

	Subelement	Total Points
FAB —	Features, Advantages, Benefits	75
WIIFM —	What's in It for Me	87
BYS —	Buying Signals	75

Find your scores for each category (FAB, WIIFM, BYS) on the following page. If your total score for any category is 80, 70, or 60, read both phrases just above and below that score). The following analysis is based on the accuracy of your selections. It reviews only the technical aspects of your selling practices.

If your responses are correct and a reflection of your actual selling performance, the following assessment will be accurate. Other critical factors that impact your selling success (for example: appearance, body language, confidence, voice, product or service knowledge, and subelements of the sale) are not factored into this study.

	Awareness Level and Probable Tendencies	
	Cornerstones of Selling Study	
	Part I — Buying Signals, What's in it for Me, and	
	Features, Advantages and Benefits	
FAB	**WIIFM**	**BYS**
80 – 100 Points		
You should be excellent at turning features into advantages and benefits. If you are also gracious, customers will like you.	It is easy for you to understand the way others think and relate to what they want to hear.	You are exceptionally perceptive. If your closing skills are as good, you will be a very successful seller.
70 – 80 Points		
You know how to use the FAB process to everyone's benefit. If you use FAB a little more often your selling success will improve.	When you want you can say the right words at the right time. Keep up the good work.	You are well aware of BYS and their importance. Listen more carefully for BYS, respond right, and begin closing more often.
60 – 70 Points		
You may be inconsistent in the way you handle FAB. This causes you to lose the opportunity of winning those difficult customers.	Your sales will increase if you think more about the buyer's needs interests and fears.	You may be unaware of missing BYS and closes but experienced buyers will be aware when you are making these mistakes.

If you scored 60 points or lower in any of these categories:

    a. Increase your knowledge of the subelement in question.

    b. Practice using the subelement in front of a mirror or with others.

    c. Video tape your roleplays and allow a qualified person to critique you.

Regardless of how well you scored, review the practices recommended in this chapter. Look for techniques that can help you, and put them to work as soon as possible.

Presenting Features, Advantages and Benefits

Customers tend to buy more, more often and sometimes at higher prices from salespeople who talk in terms the customers relate to. The *features*, *advantages and benefits* process (*FAB*) is a tool salespeople use to convert their ideas into terms that are meaningful to their customers.

Definition of FAB

FAB is the act of explaining to prospects what advantages and benefits they (their organizations or families) derive from features.

A *feature* is a component of the product or service. It can be defined as a statement regarding the salesperson's product, services or organization. For example, a copier seller might say to a prospect, "Our copier can collate multiple copies."

An *advantage* is what the feature will do for the user. For example, a copier salesperson might add, after stating the previous feature, "This collating ability can save your staff valuable time, time now spent collating papers."

A *benefit* is usually expressed as a profit or savings in time, money, effort, safety or security. It is the end reward or profit that a user will derive from the original feature. For example, the copier seller could extend the FAB process by saying, "This savings of time will save you and your organization money as well!"

Advantages and benefits are so closely related that they can often be interchanged or reversed. To qualify as an advantage or benefit, a statement must be specific and personalized. Personalizing advantages and benefits means that the salesperson must use words such as:

- You
- Your family
- Your company
- Your organization
- Or the buyer's name.

Features, advantages or benefits are of little value to either seller or prospect unless they are important to the prospect.

Purposes and Objectives of the FAB Process

The seller's purpose in using FAB are:

- To win the prospect's respect and confidence.
- To discuss those features that are most important to the prospect, stressing their corresponding advantages and benefits.
- To indicate to the prospect that the seller has listened to and understands that person's needs.
- To amplify whatever selling advantages the seller possesses.

The salesperson's FAB objectives will vary according to the selling situation. The major objectives of the FAB process are to:

- Maintain a logical approach to the selling process.
- Capitalize on the importance of any feature statement.
- Personalize the message so that it is meaningful to the prospect.

FAB is just as important to prospects as it is to sellers because:

- Prospects need to understand in simple and clear terms how features impact them (their organization and families).
- Prospects should not have to draw conclusions or guess the value of a feature.
- Without an emphasis on FAB, sellers never know if their FAB is especially interesting and valuable to prospects who:
- Are searching for a reason to buy from a vendor or salesperson.
- Are thirsting for data that will give them more product or service knowledge.

Types of FAB Statements

An appropriate FAB statement is any statement that addresses the customer's interests, needs and desires. A salesperson can use FAB in reference to the seller's:

1. Organization
   a. Size
   b. Years in business

   c. Reputation

   d. Interest in the customer

2. Service or products

   a. Quality

   b. Quantity

   c. Warranty or guarantee

   d. Durability

   e. Ease of use

   f. Multiple uses

   g. Availability

   h. Size (small, large or adjustable)

   i. Flexibility (can be used in a variety of ways or places)

   j. Trial usage

3. Terms of sale

   a. Low price

   b. Delivery terms

   c. Credit terms

   d. Money-back guarantees

   e. Exchange for other products or services if the customer is not satisfied

   f. Matching the competition's price if the price is reduced during a given period

4. After-sale support

   a. Toll-free customer service line

   b. Local customer support offices

   c. Service at buyer's location

5. Other special features

   a. Storage (moving, shipping)

   b. Customer, guest or user privileges

How to Initiate FAB

Initiating FAB is simple. Here is a step-by-step approach to the FAB process:

Step 1. The seller's *feature* statement:

"Our trucking line guarantees a much faster transit time than the one you're currently using."

Step 2. The seller's *advantage* statement (what the service or product will do for the prospect):

"This means that *your* cargo will reach its destination two days sooner than *your* present carrier can get it there. We can save *you* two valuable transit days."

Step 3. The seller's *benefits* statement (how the user will profit from the service or product):

"With us, *you* can place *your* company's merchandise in *your* stores faster, and therefore make quicker sales, and gain a faster return on *your* financial investments."

Notice how many times the words *you* and *your* appear in the previous example. The following examples demonstrate how a salesperson can turn features into advantages and benefits for a prospect:

Initiating the FAB Process
in Business-to-Business or Consumer Sales
How the Prospect Will Profit from
Dealing with the Salesperson's Customer Support Staff

Feature	Advantage	Benefit
"Our customer support staff is well-experienced."	"They will help you learn how to use the system"	"... and will save you a lot of time and effort."

How the Prospect Will Profit from
Purchasing the Salesperson's High Quality Product

Feature	Advantage	Benefit
"This product is the highest quality available."	"As a result, you will never have to replace it."	"You'll save money that others waste."

Initiating the FAB Process
in Business-to-Business Sales
How the Prospect's Organization Will
Profit from the Salesperson's Installation Program

Feature	Advantage	Benefit
"Our installation staff is well-experienced."	"They will install your group's unit quickly ..."	"...and will save your group a lot of money."

Initiating the FAB
Process in Consumer Sales
How the Prospect Will Profit from
the Salesperson's Reasonable Purchase Price

Feature	Advantage	Benefit
"Our rates are the most reasonable anywhere."	"This price advantage will save you money ..."	"...you can spend on your next vacation."
"We are having a sale on all our products."	"You save money,, and by purchasing now ..."	"you'll recieve an extra five percent discount."

When to Initiate the FAB Process

The time to initiate the FAB process is:

- Whenever the opportunity to introduce a feature that is important to the customer presents itself.
- Whenever an important feature needs to be followed up with an advantage and benefit.
- Every time a seller senses that he or she will gain some advantage with the prospect by using a FAB statement.

The successful FAB presentation relies on the salesperson making the appropriate FAB statement at the right moment. *The Anatomy of the Sale, Table 2-1* summarizes when it is appropriate to use FAB statements.

The Anatomy of the Sale
Table 2-1
Initiating FAB in the Five Steps of the Sale

Legend:

Excellent step to initiate _√√√_
Good step to initiate _√√_
Fair step to initiate _√_
Poor step to initiate_ _

The Five Steps of the Sale	Where To Initiate the FAB Process
1. Greeting	1. _ _
2. Warm-up	2. _ _
3. Qualification	3. _√√_
4. Presentation	4. _√√√_
5. Close	5. _√_

FAB Pitfalls, Causes and Options

Many salespeople sell *features*, forgetting the importance of the *advantages* and *benefits*. Consequently they miss the opportunity to capitalize on the feature by discussing its specific value to the prospect.

Prospects
do not buy features—
prospects buy benefits.

Here are the three most common mistakes salespeople make while trying to discuss FAB, why they make these mistakes and how to avoid each:

Pitfall #1—Salespeople who introduce a feature and then fail to personalize the advantages and benefits to the prospect's specific situation. In over 90 percent of the 2,500 sales roleplays my staff and I monitored for this book, sellers failed to turn features into prospect advantages and benefits. This is a common and costly error for both sellers and prospects.

If trained by technically-oriented people who lack sales and marketing experience, salespeople will typically:

- Talk in terms of features instead of benefits.
- Have a difficult time thinking like their prospects.
- Fail to understand or appreciate the value of presenting their ideas in terms that appeal to their prospects.

This problem is frequently compounded by sales managers who fail to stress the importance of interpersonal skills. Salespeople and their managers need both technical and interpersonal skills training. Salespeople must memorize and practice the use of advantages and benefits. It is a rote process that works!

Pitfall #2—Salespeople suffering from poor listening habits. Sellers who fail to listen to their prospects often do so because:

- They are not interested in what they are selling.
- They are not interested in what prospects are saying.
- They are overly concerned with what they are going to say next.

These sellers can improve their listening skills by:

- Participating in self-improvement listening courses.

- Listening for key phrases from their prospects (any phrase or word that prospects repeat or emphasize).
- Taking notes during their sales calls and responding to those issues that appear to be most important to their prospects.

Pitfall #3—Sellers insist on discussing features that are not of interest to their prospects. Salespeople who make this error usually do so because:

- They are not paying attention to their prospects' reactions.
- They do not care if their prospects are interested.
- They feel that they know more about their prospect's needs than their prospects and, therefore, continue these discussions.

These salespeople need training and development help in customer sensitivity and listening skills.

Pitfall #4—Salespeople who fail to turn product, service or vendor features into prospect benefits. These sellers are not relating to their prospects and lack the sensitivity needed to understand their prospects. Roleplaying the prospect's part with their peers will help these salespeople to:

- Develop a greater awareness of how prospects feel.
- Understand why prospects react the way they do to salespeople.

Using the WIIFM Technique

What interests prospects and customers most are issues dealing with their:

- Needs.
- Values.
- Interests.
- Concerns.
- Directions in life.
- Problems and solutions to those problems.

Definition of WIIFM

WIIFM is an acronym for the prospect's or customer's question, "What's in it for me?" In other words, how will the customer profit by purchasing the seller's products or services? The WIIFM technique is the satisfying of a customer's need to know how he or she will profit from the purchase.

Purpose and Objectives
of the WIIFM Technique

WIIFM is an excellent way to gain the customer's attention. However, it is worthless if the topics discussed are of no value to the prospect. The seller must prequalify the prospect's interest in the topics promoted, by asking if the prospect feels they are important. If the topics are unimportant, the seller must not initiate WIIFM regarding these particular topics and go on with the sale.

The purpose and objective of the WIIFM technique is to condition the salesperson to:

- Listen for the customer's needs, values, interests, concerns, directions in life, problems and solutions.
- Respond positively to the customer and explain how that person will gain (profit) from the idea, product or service offered by the seller.

WIIFM Types

WIIFM can be separated into two broad categories: *WIIFM questions* and *WIIFM statements*. A WIIFM question is any question a customer asks concerning how he or she will profit from making a given purchase. Examples of WIIFM questions follow:

- "Can I trust you?"
- "Just how good is it?"
- "Do I need your product or service?"
- "Do you know what you're talking about?"
- "How does your product or service work?"
- "How will I gain from accepting your idea?"
- "How will I profit from buying your products or services?"
- "What can your products and services do for me (or my family or organization)?"
- "Why should I change my buying practices?"
- "Why should I buy from you?"

Regardless of the nature and tone of such questions, most are firmly rooted in the question, "What's in it for me?"

Sellers naturally expect such questions from consumers or end users. Yet these types of questions also occur in business-to-business selling where the buyer (a purchasing agent or boss) may not be the user. Most business people are subtle in posing their WIIFM concerns. Some are so subtle that their vendors may not realize that the buyers are asking WIIFM questions.

Besides WIIFM questions, the prospect may challenge the seller with WIIFM statements. The prospect uses these statements to encourage the seller to explain why that prospect should buy:

- A given brand.

- From the seller.

- Because of some feature.

- A certain product or service.

- From the seller's organization.

A WIIFM statement is any statement a customer makes concerning how he or she will profit from making a given purchase. The following customer comments are examples of WIIFM statements:

- "Your price is too high."

- "Sure you have the lowest price."

- "I've heard such promises before."

- "Your promise sounds too good to be true."

- "I'm not so certain your product and services will perform as well as you claim."

- "Salespeople typically claim that their products and services are better than their competition's.

- "Vendors do not back their products and services like they promise their prospects before the sale is made."

How to Initiate WIIFM

The WIIFM technique can be initiated by sellers wherever they feel it is appropriate. They should use this technique after a prospect WIIFM question or statement by pointing out what benefits the seller offers the prospect.

Initiating the WIIFM Process in Business-to-Business Sales	Initiating the WIIFM Process in Consumer Sales
Prospect: "I've heard such promises before." **Salesperson:** "I hear the same promises. Let's review how you're protected by our company. We have a 30-day same-as-cash policy. If you don't like our service, simply cancel at any time. The service will end immediately. If you're not satisfied with our service after the free trial service period, we'll redo the work at no extra charge. It's a great deal, isn't it?"	**Prospect:** "You've got a good price." **Salesperson:** "We offer the lowest price. In fact we'll guarantee that your purchase price will be the lowest available for 30 days. If anyone dares to better our offer, just bring their ad to me. My company will refund the difference to you immediately. You have the lowest purchase price available and a work guarantee to protect you for 30 days as well. It's the kind of guarantee you'd want, isn't it?"

Initiating WIIFM

The time for a seller to initiate the WIIFM technique is right after the prospect offers a WIIFM question or statement.

The Anatomy of the Sale
Table 2-2
Initiating WIIFM
in the Five Steps of the Sale

Legend:

Excellent step to initiate _√√√_
Good step to initiate _√√_
Fair step to initiate _√_
Poor step to initiate_ _

The Five Steps of the Sale	Where To Initiate the WIIFM Process
1. Greeting	1. _ _
2. Warm-up	2. _ _
3. Qualification	3. _√√_
4. Presentation	4. _√√√_
5. Close	5. _√√√_

WIIFM Pitfall, Cause and Option

Here is an example of a pitfall salespeople encounter when attempting to use WIIFM.

Pitfall—The salespeople do not respond to WIIFM opportunities. The sellers may fail to respond because they may:

• Not know how to prepare themselves for WIIFM opportunities.

• Lack experience in recognizing or answering WIIFM opportunities.

• Not hear (or know how to identify) their prospects' WIIFM opportunities.

To overcome these challenges, sellers should:

• Develop a written series of WIIFM opportunities and example statements.

- Review and study commonly heard WIIFM questions and statements until the sellers recognize them easily.
- Roleplay the part of a prospect with their peers until they become more adept at using WIIFM statements.

Recognizing Buying Signals

Buying signals are an important aspect of the selling process. They are the buyer's way of saying, "I am (or may be) ready to buy."

Sellers who are successful in their use of the FAB and WIIFM processes will hear their prospects respond occasionally with buying signals. To be effective in closing, salespeople must understand:

- What a buying signal is.
- A buying signal's importance to both buyers and sellers.
- How to respond to a prospect's buying signal.

Definition of a Buying Signal

A buying signal is any show of interest on the customer's part in the product, the service, terms of purchase or the seller's organization.

Purposes and Objectives of a Buying Signal

Buying signals are a prospect's way of indicating to a seller that it may be time to reach some kind of agreement. Once a seller hears a buying signal the objectives are to:

- Test the prospect's interest by making a closing statement or offering a closing question.
- Immediately complete the transaction if possible.

Types of Buying Signals

There are *weak* and *strong* (legitimate) buying signals. A strong buying signal means that the prospect is asking questions because of a sincere interest in buying the product or service. A weak buying signal means that the prospect is curious but not necessarily interested in making a purchase.

1. Below are examples of strong (legitimate) buying signals.

- "I'll take it."

- "Write it up."

- "Send it to me tomorrow."

- "I don't know whether this will fit in the space available."

- "Send me a proposal that I can take to the purchasing committee."

- "Can you help me sell this to my wife (husband, boss or organization)?"

2. The following statements are examples of weak buying signals that need to be tested.

   - "Do you have a credit plan?"

   - "What's the minimum order?"

   - "I like your product or service."

   - "Is it available in any other colors?"

   - "What does your warranty plan cover?"

   - "Yes, but will you be there if I have a problem?"

   - "What do you think?" The prospect is seeking advice about making a purchase.

   - "You're a good salesperson." (The seller should take care in responding to this type of compliment as some customers use such praise to manipulate salespeople.)

How to Evaluate and Respond To or Test a Buying Signal

Since trial closes are the only way to test a prospect's interest, professionally trained salespeople are taught to close on buying signals. A buying signal is a closing opportunity. Sellers must understand that many buying signals call for some statement from the salesperson before that seller attempts to close the prospect. The only way for a salesperson to determine if a buying signal is legitimate is to counter with a question or direct statement.

Initiating a
Buying Signal Response
in Business-to-Business or Consumer Sales

A prospect's question followed by a *high-risk* question—

Prospect: "How much is that unit?"

Salesperson: "How much do you want to spend?"

A prospect's question followed by a direct answer and a *low-risk* close—

Prospect: "How much is that unit?"

Salesperson: "We are asking twenty thousand. Are you interested in *looking* at it?"

A prospect's question followed by a direct answer and a *high-risk* close—

Prospect: "How much is that unit?"

Salesperson: "We're asking twenty thousand. Are you interested in *buying* it?"

A prospect's question followed by a direct answer and a *low-risk* question—

Prospect: "How much is that unit?"

Salesperson: "We're asking twenty thousand. Is that about what you wanted to spend?"

**An *overt* or *strong buying signal*
followed by a direct response and a choice close—**

Prospect: "How soon could I expect delivery?"

Salesperson: "Thursday or Friday. Which day is better for you?"

**An example of a *weak buying signal*
followed by a direct response and a question—**

Prospect: "How much will your services cost us monthly?"

Salesperson: "$550 per month. Does that fit your budget?"

When To Respond to a Buying Signal

A salesperson should respond to a buying signal the moment a prospect indicates an interest in the product, service, terms of sale or seller's organization. The longer the salesperson takes in responding to the signal:

• The weaker the impact of a response.

• The less likely the seller will close successfully.

The Anatomy of the Sale
Table 2-3
When Buying Signals Occur
During the Five Steps of the Sale

Legend:

Most frequently occur _√√√_
Sometimes occur _√√_
Rarely occur _√_
Never occur_ _

The Five Steps of the Sale	Where Buying Signals Typically Occur
1. Greeting	1. _ _
2. Warm-up	2. _√_
3. Qualification	3. _√√√_
4. Presentation	4. _√√√_
5. Close	5. _√√_

Buying Signal Pitfalls, Causes and Options

Here are a few examples of the kinds of pitfalls salespeople encounter with buying signals:

Pitfall #1—Sellers may suffer from poor listening habits. Poor listening habits are sometimes caused by:

- Laziness.
- Lack of training.
- Lack of interest in making a sale.
- Lack of interest in the customer as a person.
- Lack of concern with their prospects' needs.

Sellers wanting to overcome this kind of challenge should:

- Make a conscientious effort to listen to what their prospects are saying.
- Make brief notes during the sales call of their prospects' key issues.

- Take a listening course or read a book about how to improve this vital skill.
- Reevaluate their goals and commitments and make certain that their conduct is in line with their objectives.

Pitfall #2—Sellers recognize buying signals but fail to respond to them. Failing to respond to buying signals can be caused by the sellers':

- Fear of rejection.
- Poor self-images.
- Fear of asserting themselves.
- Fear of creating negative situations with prospects.

To better handle these fears salespeople should:

- Seek assistance from qualified people who can help them understand and overcome these handicaps.
- Remember that they have everything to gain and nothing to lose by responding to their prospects' buying signals.
- Realize that all salespeople (successful, unsuccessful, new and experienced) face the same obstacles and challenges.
- Recognize that those prospects who reject sellers' recommendations normally are rejecting ideas, products, services or terms of sale—not the salesperson.
- Remind themselves that their purpose in meeting with their prospects is to help the prospects fill their needs. The seller has an obligation to ask closing questions if those needs can be filled through the purchase of the sellers' products or services.
- Consider that these fears may result from lack of closing experience. Overcoming these fears can be achieved by the salespeople practicing their responses to buying signals and closing until they are:
  - Comfortable with responding to buying signals.
  - Confident in their ability to close their prospects.

Pitfall #3—The seller is unable to recognize buying signals. The inability to recognize buying signals is caused by:

- A lack of training.
- A lack of experience.

The solutions for avoiding this pitfall and remedying its causes are training and roleplaying in:

- How to identify buying signals.
- How to close.
- How to deal with a prospect's objections and rejections.

Chapter Summary

1. *FAB* is an acronym for features, advantages and benefits.
2. *FAB* is the act of explaining to prospects what advantages and benefits they (their organizations or families) will derive from features.
3. A *feature* is a statement regarding your product, service, staff or organization.
4. An *advantage* is what the feature will do for its user.
5. A *benefit* is the end reward or profit that its user will derive from a feature.
6. Customers do not buy features—customers buy benefits.
7. Advantages and benefits are so closely related that they can often be interchanged.
8. A *feature* is a general statement (regarding your product, service, staff or organization). An advantage or a benefit, (to qualify as an advantage or a benefit) must be specific and personalized.
9. Personalizing advantages and benefits means that the salesperson must use words and phrases such as:
    *   You
    *   Your family
    *   Your company
    *   Your organization
    *   Or the buyer's name.
10. The time to initiate the FAB process is:
    *   Whenever the opportunity presents itself to introduce a feature that is important to the customer.
    *   Whenever an important feature is mentioned and can be followed up with an advantage and benefit.
    *   Every time you sense that you will gain some advantage with the client by using a FAB statement.
11. *WIIFM* is an acronym for the customer asking, "What's in it for me?"
12. The *WIIFM* process is the satisfying of a customer's need to know how he or she will profit from the purchase.
13. *WIIFM* can be separated into two broad categories; *WIIFM questions* and *WIIFM statements*.

14. *WIIFM questions* are questions customers ask concerning how they will profit from making a given purchase.

15. *WIIFM statements* are comments customers make referring to how they will profit from making a given purchase.

16. A seller should initiate the WIIFM technique immediately after the customer offers a WIIFM question or statement.

17. *Buying signals* are closing opportunities. They are ways the buyer indicates to the seller that it may be time to reach an agreement.

18. A *buying signal* is any show of interest on the customer's part in your products, services, terms of purchase or your employer's organization.

19. A *strong* (legitimate) *buying signal* is an indication that the prospect is sincerely interested in buying a product or service.

20. A *weak buying signal* means that the prospect is curious but not necessarily interested in making a purchase.

21. When you hear a *buying signal*, respond appropriately and then trial close.

3

The First Two
Steps in Sales Negotiations—
Asking the Right Questions
and Handling Objections

*Every time a buyer says
yes, a selling opportunity
exists. Every time a buyer says
no, there exists an opportunity to make a
sale. There are no guarantees that a prospect
will or will not buy—only selling opportunities.*

"Good afternoon," the salesperson greeted us in a somber fashion.

"Hello," I replied.

"Looking for a personal computer?" he asked.

"Yes."

"Well, we've got the best," he assured me as he raced into his next thought. "Let me show you what I mean. Here are several models from one of the largest computer manufacturers in the world. You'll like what they can do," he said, and then paused for a gasp of air.

"They all look very nice," I interjected.

"Which one would you like?" he asked.

Which one would I like? I wondered silently. *I don't know what these boxes can do. I don't know the prices. I don't even know what I need. How can I give him an answer?*

"I don't know," I replied.

"They're nice looking aren't they?"

"Yes, but I don't know what they do," I insisted.

"Oh, they do it all," he replied quickly. "Especially this one—it's built by the best computer manufacturer in the world. We're directly owned by them. It's the best computer on the market."

He raved on for another two or three minutes about his employer, service and quality without ever asking what I needed.

Out of boredom I asked, "How much does this one cost?"

After he replied I observed, "This is one of the most expensive personal computers I've seen."

"Yes, it is expensive," he replied.

"Does the manufacturer justify the price?" I asked

"Well, you get what you pay for," he answered defensively, failing to further address the issue.

"Is it a multi-tasking and multi-user system?" I inquired.

"No. If that's what you need, this machine won't do it'" he stated firmly, assuming that I needed a multi-tasking, multi-user machine—which I didn't.

He's sure to ask me a few questions and then we'll proceed. I thought. But he didn't.

"Well, nice meeting you," he said without any feeling of sincerity as he walked away.

I was stunned and kept asking myself, *Why didn't he just ask a few simple questions? Maybe together we could figure out what I need. He must be new in sales*.

The computer salesperson made a fundamental mistake that afternoon—he failed to do his job. He failed to examine my needs and handle my questions in a professional way. An important part of selling is knowing what questions to ask, when to ask them, and how to ask those questions.

Sometimes, asking the right questions is critical to helping the buyer better understand what type of purchase they should be considering. Asking the right questions is vital to the seller's understanding of what the customer needs and how to address those needs.

Professionally handling customer objections is just as important to selling as asking the right questions. Both subjects, *how to ask questions* and *how to handle objections*, are addressed in this chapter.

Evaluating Your Understanding of the Cornerstones of Selling

Part II—Asking Questions and Handling Objections

Before reading further, you may desire to examine your awareness of these two subjects. For that reason we have included a self-assessment exercise here. If you have not read the instructions that precede the self-assessment exercise in Chapter 2, you might review them at this time. These sections are titled *Evaluating Your Understanding of the Cornerstones of Selling* and *Exercise Suggestions*.

Exercise

Cornerstones of Selling Study
Part II—Asking Questions and Handling Objections

Instructions:

Check the letter next to the answer that is most accurate. Please mark only one selection for each question. For example:

> 0. I like to sell to:
>   a. New prospects.
>   b. People I know.
> √ c. It doesn't matter.

In making your selections:

- Do not mark any phrase you are uncertain of or that does not apply.
- Check the *Glossary* or *Index* for any word that is unfamiliar.
- Be as honest as possible, and mark the way you actually perform or behave.

This is a continuation of the Cornerstones of Selling Study Exercise. This section begins with number 31.

31. After I greet the prospect:

    a. My first questions deal with the purpose of our meeting.

    b. My first questions deal with nonbusiness related issues.

    c. I rarely ask questions as I begin my presentation.

32. In asking questions, I am aware of the impact of my voice:

    a. Yes, I consciously vary its pitch, depth and volume.

    b. No, I rarely monitor its pitch, depth and volume.

    c. Sometimes I am aware of its impact.

33. In a selling situation, I use my questions:

    a. In a logical and systematic fashion.

    b. As it occurs to me to use them.

    c. Sometimes logically and sometimes spontaneously.

34. My prospects would say my sales-related questions generally:

    a. Vary according to my mood.

    b. Are off-the-cuff and spontaneous.

    c. Are goal-oriented, focused and premeditated.

35. I am well-prepared to question my prospects:

    a. Yes, and I adjust my questioning style as necessary.

    b. It all depends on the selling situation.

    c. I don't rehearse this process.

36. When I ask my prospects difficult questions:

    a. I avoid looking them in the eyes so as not to intimidate them.

    b. I look directly at them, trying to establish eye contact:

    c. My eye contact varies with the selling situation.

37. When asking questions, I am aware of my body language:

    a. Yes, I consciously vary it to achieve the impact I desire.

    b. No, I rarely consciously vary it to achieve any impact.

    c. Sometimes I consciously vary it to achieve impact.

38. I am more likely to use leading questions in the:

    a. Initial stages of my sale.

    b. Later stages of my sale.

    c. I do not use leading questions.

39. I am more likely to use probing or closed questions in the:

    a. Information-gathering stage of my sale.

    b. Presentation stage of my sale.

    c. I do not use probing or closed questions.

40. I am more likely to use general or open questions in the:

    a. Initial stages of my sale.

    b. Later stages of my sale.

    c. I do not use general or open questions.

41. "How are you?" is a:

    a. Leading question.

    b. Specific or closed question.

    c. General or open question.

42. "Are you going to make a purchase today?" is a:

    a. Leading question.

    b. Specific or closed question.

    c. General or open question.

43. "This is the best price you've been quoted isn't it?", is a:

    a. Leading question.

    b. Probing or closed question.

    c. General or open question.

44. "Do you want three or four of these?" is a:

    a. Leading question.

    b. Probing question.

    c. General or open question.

45. "Is that your final offer?" is a:

    a. Leading question.

    b. Specific or closed question.

    c. General or open question.

46. I think of objections as:

    a. Positive.

    b. Negative.

    c. Something a salesperson has to endure.

47. I normally react to hostile objections:

    a. Rapidly.

    b. As the situation merits.

    c. I rarely react or respond to hostile objections.

48. I generally react to hostile objections as if:

    a. The objections are aimed at me personally.

    b. The objections are part of a debate.

    c. I am trying to help the objecting party overcome a problem or challenge.

49. I think of and react to objections as:

    a. Problem solving challenges.

    b. Selling opportunities.

    c. Tasks I have to deal with.

50. With irate customers I am usually:

    a. Nonresponsive.

    b. Aggressive.

    c. Patient.

51. When a prospect objects to one of my suggestions I normally:

    a. Respond immediately.

    b. Ask the prospect a question to help clarify the objection.

    c. Give the prospect my best answer.

52. My reaction to prospects who challenge me continuously is to:

    a. Avoid them.

    b. Challenge them just as aggressively.

    c. Vary my style so they can't predict my next move.

53. In handling objections, I preplan my use of questions:

    a. Yes, I often counter customer objections with questions.

    b. I use questions in handling objections but I do not plan.

    c. I do not counter a customer's objections with questions.

54. My prospects would rate my handling of difficult objections as:
    a. Excellent.
    b. Good.
    c. Fair.

55. In dealing with a customer's objections I normally use:
    a. A couple basic methods I feel confident with.
    b. A variety of techniques—over five different ones if needed.
    c. I cannot objectively evaluate my handling of objections.

56. "I'm not buying since your last ten deliveries were late." is:
    a. A valid objection.
    b. A visceral objection.
    c. An imaginary objection.

57. "I'm not going to buy since something may go wrong." is:
    a. An intellectual objection.
    b. A personal objection.
    c. An excuse.

58. "I hate your company and disdain its service policies." is:
    a. A valid objection.
    b. A visceral objection.
    c. An imaginary objection.

59. "I'm not buying because I don't have enough data yet." is:
    a. An intellectual objection.
    b. A personal objection.
    c. A visceral objection.

60. "I'm not buying because I don't like working with you." is:
    a. An intellectual objection.
    b. A personal objection.
    c. An imaginary objection.

Scoring

Cornerstones of Selling Study
Part II—Asking Questions and Handling Objections

Legend

AQ   —   Asking Questions.
HO   —   Handling Objections.

Instructions:

From the previous *Exercise*, circle the same letters below, including the score. After completing this section, proceed to the *Score Box*. Make certain your answers reflect the way you actually interact with your prospects and customers.

31. After I greet the prospect:

   a. 0

   b. 6   AQ

   c. 0

32. In asking questions, I am aware of the impact of my voice:

   a. 6   AQ

   b. 0

   c. 3   AQ

33. In a selling situation, I use my questions:

   a. 6   AQ

   b. 0

   c. 3   AQ

34. My prospects would say my sales-related questions generally:

   a. 0

   b. 0

   c. 6   AQ

35. I am well-prepared to question my prospects:

    a. 6   AQ

    b. 0

    c. 0

36. When I ask my prospects difficult questions:

    a. 0

    b. 6   AQ

    c. 3   AQ

37. When asking questions, I am aware of my body language:

    a. 6   AQ

    b. 0

    c. 3   AQ

38. I am more likely to use leading questions in the:

    a. 3   AQ

    b. 6   AQ

    c. 0

39. I am more likely to use probing or closed questions in the:

    a. 6   AQ

    b. 3   AQ

    c. 0

40. I am more likely to use general or open questions in the:

    a. 6   AQ

    b. 0

    c. 0

41. "How are you?" is a:

    a. 0

    b. 0

    c. 6   AQ

42. "Are you going to make a purchase today?" is a:

    a. 0

    b. 6   AQ

    c. 0

43. "This is the best price you have been quoted' isn't it?" is a:

    a. 6   AQ

    b. 3   AQ

    c. 0

44. "Do you want three or four of these?" is a:

    a. 3   AQ

    b. 6   AQ

    c. 0

45. "Is that your final offer?" is a:

    a. 0

    b. 6   AQ

    c. 0

46. I think of objections as:

    a. 6   HO

    b. 0

    c. 0

47. I normally react to hostile objections:

    a. 0

    b. 6   HO

    c. 0

48. I generally react to hostile objections as if:

    a. 0

    b. 0

    c. 6   HO

49. I think of and react to objections as:

    a. 6   HO

    b. 6   HO

    c. 0

50. With irate customers I am usually:

    a. 0

    b. 0

    c. 6   HO

51. When a prospect objects to one of my suggestions I normally:

    a. 0

    b. 6   HO

    c. 0

52. My reaction to prospects who challenge me continuously:

    a. 0

    b. 0

    c. 6   HO

53. In handling objections, I preplan my use of questions:

    a. 6   HO

    b. 3   HO

    c. 0

54. My prospects would rate my handling of difficult objections as:

    a. 6   HO

    b. 3   HO

    c. 1   HO

55. In dealing with a customer's objections I normally use:

    a. 3   HO

    b. 6   HO

    c. 0

56. "I'm not buying since your last ten deliveries were late." is:

    a. 6   HO

    b. 0

    c. 0

57. "I'm not going to buy since something may go wrong." is:

    a. 0

    b. 0

    c. 6   HO

58. "I hate your company and disdain its service policies." is:

    a. 0

    b. 6   HO

    c. 0

59. "I'm not buying because I don't have enough data yet:" is:

    a. 6   HO

    b. 0

    c. 0

60. "I'm not buying because I don't like working with you." is:

    a. 0

    b. 6   HO

    c. 0

Score Box
Cornerstones of Selling Study
Part II—Asking Questions and Handling Objections
Instructions:

Total your score for each category and place it on the line to the right of the appropriate classification. Then add 10 points to determine your total score:

	Subelement	Points Scored		Total Points
AQ	— Asking Questions	_____	+ 10 points =	_____
HO	— Handling Objections	_____	+ 10 points =	_____

Find your scores for each category (AQ, HO) on the following page. If your total score for any category is 80, 70, or 60, read both phrases (just above and below that score). The following analysis is based on the accuracy of your selections. It reviews only the technical aspects of your selling practices.

If your responses are correct and a reflection of your actual selling performance, the following assessment will be accurate. Other critical factors that impact your selling success (for example: appearance, body language, confidence, voice, product, or service knowledge, and subelements of the sale) are not factored into this study.

Awareness Level and Probable Tendencies
Cornerstones of Selling Study
Part II — Asking Questions and Handling Objections

AQ	HO
80 – 100 Points	
You have a keen awareness of the importance of this skill. If you are proficient in using this data, you are or will become an exceptional information gatherer.	You are a proactive seller, as you anticipate and know how to deal with objections. You have a good attitude toward objections. Hostile prospects should not upset you easily.
70 – 80 Points	
You are more knowledgeable than most sellers in this area. If you use your knowledge in a consistent fashion it will help you become more successful in sales.	You know how to handle prospect objections. Like the top-rated sellers in this category, it will be difficult for others to upset you. You probably have a positive response to most objections.
60 – 70 Points	
Some prospects will give you a good or passing score in this area while others will rightfully claim that you are not sensitive enough to their needs or interests.	While you understand some of the basics in handling prospect objections your performance in this area is erratic. You can become defensive if confronted by hostile or challenging prospects.

If you scored 60 points or lower in any of these categories:

    a.   Increase your knowledge of the subelement in question.

    b.   Practice using the subelement in front of a mirror or with others.

    c.   Video tape your roleplays and allow a qualified person to critique you.

Regardless of how well you scored, review the practices recommended in this chapter. Look for those techniques that can help you, and put them to work as soon as possible.

How to Ask Questions

Questioning is a necessary sales function. It is one that must be appropriately timed and structured. Overwhelming prospects with too many questions, leaving them little time to answer, can be fatal to the sale. Likewise, asking questions that are irrelevant to the prospect can needlessly annoy that person or destroy the flow of the sale. Sellers must know:

- How to ask questions.
- How to phrase their questions.
- How the questions fit within the steps of the sale.
- How to use questions to establish good rapport with prospects.
- How to gather the information needed to make a presentation and close the deal.

Randomly asking questions will not make a salesperson effective. Such a lack of structure broadcasts to the customer that the seller is unprepared to handle the sale. Asking the right questions at the right moments allows salespeople to demonstrate their:

- Professionalism.
- Resourcefulness.
- Organizational skills.
- Thoroughness of thought.
- Respect for their prospects and their prospects' time.

Those who intend to be successful in sales must handle their prospects' and customers' questions efficiently and effectively. There are several different kinds of questions and each has specific uses. Understanding the differences in each question group and how to best use and position them is an important part of selling. This section deals with seller-generated questions.

Definition of a Question

Since this book deals with the cornerstones of selling, this definition is specific to the sales profession: a sales question helps the seller gather information or lead a prospect to some conclusion.

Purposes and Objectives of Question Groups

Salesperson's questions should be thought of as selling tools. Sellers must learn to ask their questions skillfully. Questioning skills are essential to gathering information, buying time to think and position one's ideas.

The skillful use of questions assists sellers in:

- Closing sales.
- Creating confidence.
- Planning sales strategies.
- Validating prospects' needs.
- Reconfirming statements or issues.
- Guiding prospects through the sale.
- Leading prospects to some conclusion.
- Gaining information necessary for the sale.
- Using selling time with prospects efficiently.
- Building rapport and understanding with prospects.
- Overcoming prospect objections, fears or hidden hostilities.

Types of Questions

There are basic patterns regarding the creation and use of questions. In sales there are four basic question groups from which salespeople develop their questions:

1. *General* or *open* questions
2. *Reflective* or *probing* questions
3. *Specific* or *closed* questions
4. *Leading* questions

A review of these question types follows.

1. General or Open Questions

General questions offer the prospect a wide range of responses. They often call for an opinion or feeling. These questions should get the prospect involved and talking.

Open questions offer certain advantages to the salesperson, especially during the warm-up and qualification stages of selling. They encourage the prospect to:

- Express:
    - Fears
    - Needs
    - Beliefs
    - Interests
    - Feelings
    - Opinions
    - Concerns
- Respond openly and nondefensively.
- Become actively involved in the selling process.
- Uncover areas of personal interest and needs.
- Provide the seller with information about the prospect, such as the prospect's:
    - Interests
    - Family
    - Superiors
    - Employer

It should be noted that open questions can also be time consuming and allow the salesperson or prospect to wander away from the objectives of the meeting.

Open questions are effective for gathering general data. Therefore, they are typically used by the seller in the first three steps of the sale (greeting, warm-up, qualification). They can be used in response to objections and to uncover problem areas that may exist. They may also be used to:

- Increase the prospect's sense of worth.
- Stimulate rapport between seller and prospect.
- Elicit information from the prospect in a nonthreatening fashion.

How to Initiate General or Open Questions

Initiating general or open questions can be difficult for introverted or novice sellers since casual conversation is somewhat difficult for these people. However, using this type of question is simple and becomes easy with practice.

Writing and practicing the kinds of questions a seller would ask during a sales call makes the process easy.

Common sense is a vital part of selling. So when it comes to asking questions, a seller's queries should be relevant to the process at hand. Here are several examples of general or open questions a salesperson can use with a customer or prospect:

Initiating General or Open Questions in Business-to-Business Sales	Initiating General or Open Questions in Consumer Sales
• "How are you?" • "How large is your company?" • "How long have you been with the company?" • "How long have you been in this location?" • "Is your job much different from your past position?"	• "How are you?" • "How large is your family?" • "How long have you been married?" • "How long have you lived at your present address?" • "Is this community much different from the one you lived in before?"

2. Reflective or Probing Questions

Reflective questions explore a prospect's response more thoroughly. These questions encourage feedback through the seller's restatement, paraphrasing and mirroring a prospect's responses. These questions probe the prospect, asking for more detailed explanation. Used with open questions, reflective questions can help the seller gain more information.

How to Initiate Reflective or Probing Questions

Examples of reflective or probing questions a salesperson can use with a prospect are listed below:

Initiating Reflective or Probing Questions in Business-to-Business Sales	Initiating Reflective or Probing Questions in Consumer Sales
• "Will your boss approve of this action?" • "Are you satisfied with your present vendor's service?" • "Are you and your boss happy with your old ____ (name product)?"	• "Will your spouse approve of this action?" • "Are you satisfied with your present vendor's service?" • "Are you and your spouse happy with your old ____ (name product)?"

These questions call for prospects to rethink their positions and may reveal needs previously unstated or not thought out. Use of the reflective question can:

- Clarify a point.
- Improve understanding.
- Expand on an idea or feeling.
- Reopen discussion and thought.
- Avoid hurried, inaccurate conclusions.

The overuse of this type of question causes customers to feel that the sellers are mimicking their responses.

3. Specific or Closed Questions

Specific questions call for specific answers. They give the seller control over the conversation, while limiting the customer's range of responses.

Prospects may view this type of question as forceful, since it is so direct and to the point. Sellers should therefore use closed questions in a positive framework with sensitivity and good timing. Such questions are frequently used to the seller's advantage during the presentation and closing to:

- Trial close.
- Guide the prospect.
- Call for a decision from the prospect.
- Provide the seller with a summation guide.

- Test the prospect's intentions or level of commitment.
- Provide the seller with a way to reconfirm points of agreement.

Exclusive use of closed questions may produce a cross-examination effect, causing the customer to feel defensive. If used excessively, it also may prevent the seller from gaining necessary insight and block effective communication. Customers may feel that the sellers are manipulating them. Nevertheless, closed questioning is an effective tool when used wisely.

How to Initiate Specific or Closed Questions

Salespeople use specific or closed questions more often than they realize. Here are some examples of specific or closed questions:

Initiating Specific or Closed Questions in Business-to-Business Sales	Initiating Specific or Closed Questions in Consumer Sales
• "Do you want it sent on Monday or Tuesday?"	• "Do you want it sent on Monday or Tuesday?"
• "Does your company want to pay in installments or one lump sum?"	• "Would you like to pay in installments or one lump sum?"
• "Will a purchasing committee have to review this transaction?"	• "Will you have to discuss this transaction with your spouse?"

4. Leading Questions

Leading questions help the seller guide the customer to some conclusion. The use of leading questions is normally a premeditated act. A leading question can easily be used in the closing stages of the sale as follows:

- "Well, you're interested in the best services available for your company, aren't you?"

>   or

- "You would only want to work with a vendor who can supply you in a timely fashion, wouldn't you?"

How to Initiate Leading Questions

Leading questions are common and easy to use. Here are some examples of leading questions:

Initiating Leading Questions in Business-to-Business Sales	Initiating Leading Questions in Consumer Sales
• "This is what you and your boss requested, isn't it?" • "You did say that you wanted the lowest price possible, didn't you?"	• "This is what you and your family requested, isn't it?" • "You did say that you wanted the lowest price possible, didn't you?"
Leading Statement	
• "As you know, industry rates are going up this quarter."	• "As you know, everyone's prices are increasing soon."

Regarding the last two examples, the customer may or may not know that prices are rising. However, the salesperson is using this leading statement to get agreement or to put the customer in an indefensible position. The latter is a manipulative act. It can be effective with those who lack the confidence to rebuke the assumptive and leading statement:

Initiating Questions

A seller uses questions to:

- Clarify an issue.
- Gather information.
- Plant information.
- Intimidate a customer.
- Guide the listener to a given point.
- Draw the customer's attention to some issue.
- Test the customer's readiness to make a buying decision.
- Box in, or trap, the customer into agreeing with the salesperson.

Depending on the speaker's vocal inflection and choice of words, leading questions can be reassuring, nonthreatening, or intimidating.

"It's all in the timing," is an appropriate motto for this section. Questions should be used to address the needs of those involved in the selling and buying process. *The Anatomy of the Sale, Table 3-1* demonstrates where, when, and what types of questions to use in each step of the sale.

The Anatomy of the Sale Table 3-1 Initiating the Various Types of Questions During the Five Steps of a Sale	
The Five Steps of the Sale	**What Type of Questions to Initiate**
1. Greeting	1. General or Open Questions
2. Warm-up	2. General or Open Questions
3. Qualification	3. General or Open, Specific or Closed, Reflective or Probing Questions
4. Presentation	4. Leading Questions
5. Close	5. Leading, Specific or Closed Questions

Question Pitfalls, Causes and Options

Here are a few examples of the kinds of pitfalls sellers encounter while asking questions:

Pitfall #1—A lack of planning and organization can cause the salesperson to ask inappropriate questions. It can also cause a seller to forget to ask necessary questions. This error results from laziness or poor time-management skills. A lack of planning and organization can be overcome but it takes time, effort and drive. Sellers who need help in these areas must study their products, services, organizations, markets, industries and customer base. They must learn how to anticipate asking the kind of questions needed to:

- Get the necessary data.

- Lead the customer to some conclusion or to the close.

Pitfall #2—A lack of practice and discipline in how to ask questions can lead to inappropriate or ineffective questions. A lack of practice usually results from lack of discipline and training. To learn how to deal with prospect questions, sellers need to gather the necessary information. Therefore, salespeople should write questions that customers frequently ask, with appropriate responses. They then can practice replying to these prospect questions with a peer, a friend or a mirror.

Pitfall #3—Lack of thought and analysis can cause salespeople to make sloppy, incompetent, and disorganized qualifications and presentations. A lack of analysis may indicate a lack of interest, on the seller's part, in making the sale. Salespeople desiring to overcome these challenges should ask themselves:

- Why they are having these problems?

- Do they want to do anything about these challenges?

- What they must do to overcome these obstacles?

- Are they are willing to make the sacrifice needed to improve their attitudes and selling styles?

- When are they going to begin making the necessary changes?

From this point they must practice and execute what they have learned.

How to Handle Objections

Salespeople must understand that the prospect has a right to make an *objection*. Just as the prospect has the right to make an objection, the seller has a right, and sometimes an obligation, to respond to a prospect's objection.

Some salespeople are afraid of objections and rejection. Fearing rejection and objections is natural since they never know when, where, or how a customer may object to their ideas. This makes it difficult, but not impossible, to plan effective responses. Salespeople who know their products and services and how to handle objections normally have nothing to fear.

Definition of an Objection

An objection is any statement a prospect or customer gives for refusing the seller's employer, product, services, ideas, price, or terms of sale.

Purpose and Objectives of Handling Objections in a Professional Fashion

The purpose of this section is to help salespeople understand that objections are a natural part of the selling process and there are effective ways to handle them. Salespeople's objectives in this area are:

- To help their prospect clarify their objection (if necessary).
- To identify the cause of their prospect's objections (if not evident).
- To select ways to handle the objections.

Types of Objections

Objections can be grouped into six categories:

1. *Intellectual* objections
2. *Personal* objections
3. *Visceral* objections
4. *Imaginary* objections
5. *Valid* objections
6. *Excuses*

1. Intellectual Objections

An intellectual objection is one in which the prospect objects to the seller on a mental (theoretical) level. Personality differences and emotions are not the cause of these objections.

2. Personal Objections

A personal objection reflects the prospect's emotional reactions to the seller's personality, product, service or organization. The reaction may not always be obvious to others.

3. Visceral Objections

A visceral objection is a hostile objection that also may be:

- Antagonistic

- Malicious

- Vengeful

A difficult situation for the seller to deal with is a prospect who has become a visceral opponent. Once alienated, that prospect is no longer open to listening, communicating and buying. In such cases, the prospect may even view the seller as an adversary. Although many visceral objections are obvious, some prospects can hide their feelings well.

4. Imaginary Objections

An imaginary objection is a rejection without any tangible or logical basis. For example:

- "Your price is too high," when the prospect does not know what a fair market price is for that product or service.

- "You can't meet our needs," when the prospect has no idea whether the seller can meet his or her needs.

An imaginary objection is usually illogical or otherwise invalid. It often happens when the prospect:

- Is over-anxious or fears that something may go wrong.

- Is disappointed over similar past situations.

5. Valid Objections

Except for imaginary objections or excuses, any of the other kinds of objections can be valid objections. A valid objection is any objection that may have merit.

6. Excuses

An excuse is a rationalization a prospect uses to avoid making a decision or statement. A prospect may use an excuse when that person:
- Is confused.
- Is lying or hiding something.
- Is afraid to make a commitment.
- Does not want to make a decision.
- Wants to avoid openly rejecting the seller.

How to Respond to Objections

How a salesperson can best respond to an objection depends greatly upon the:
- Time constraints.
- Seller's personality.
- Prospect's personality.
- Competitive situation (if any).
- Selling environment (adversarial or collaborative).

There are many ways a seller can respond to an objection. *The Five Classic Ways to Respond to Customer Objections* are:

1. Answer the objection directly with a statement.
2. Answer the objection with a question or series of questions, and then address the objection.
3. Allow the customer to handle his or her objection in response to your asking leading questions.
4. Extinguish the issue by not responding to the customer's objection.
5. Agree with the customer.

Responding to the prospect's objection with a solution is not always to the salesperson's advantage, especially when that response:
- Does not suit the buyer.
- Makes the seller sound defensive.
- Does not answer the prospect's objection.

One way sellers can respond to prospects' objections is by seeking greater clarification regarding the prospects' problems. Salespeople must get their prospects to quantify and qualify the reasons they are objecting. The more knowledge sellers have regarding their prospects' objections, the better chance they have of successfully handling the objections.

Qualitative Questions

Qualitative questions are indirect queries. Usually these questions deal with nontangible information such as feelings, thoughts and emotions. Qualifying an objection means encouraging prospects to express their feelings about why they are offering an objection.

The following sample questions encourage prospects to clarify their objections and their feelings.

Initiating Qualitative Questions in Handling Objections in Business-to-Business Sales or Consumer Sales

Examples of qualitative questions—

a.   *Prospect:*   "Your price is too high."
      Seller: "Why do you think that?"

b.   *Prospect:*   "Your delivery time is too slow."
      Seller: "What makes you say that?"

c.   *Prospect:*   "Your service isn't as good as it should be."
      Seller: "Please explain that feeling."

Quantitative Questions

Quantitative questions are direct queries that call for specific responses. Usually these questions deal with tangible things such as facts, figures, sources, times, places and dates. Quantifying an objection means encouraging prospects to back their objections with facts.

The following sample questions encourage prospects to quantify their objections.

Initiating Quantitative Questions in Handling Objections in Business-to-Business Sales or Consumer Sales

Examples of quantitative questions—

a. *Prospect:* "Your price is too high."
   Seller: "By what amount?"
   or
   Seller: "In comparison to what?"

b. *Prospect:* "Your delivery time is too slow."
   Seller: "Does someone else offer a quicker delivery?"
   Prospect: "Yes."
   Seller: "What delivery time would you like?"

c. *Prospect:* "Your service isn't as good as it should be."
   Seller: "What type of service do you want?"
   or
   Seller: "What's missing from our service?"

Quantitative questions can sometimes put the prospect on the defensive. Sellers who put prospects on the defensive are taking a great risk in doing so, since most people do not like sellers who pressure them and prospects will rarely buy when they feel defensive. Prospects also tend to dislike salespeople who make them feel inferior and will avoid dealing with such sellers in the future.

Extinguishment (not responding to prospects' objections) can be effective or dangerous. The seller must have a solid grasp of how important a customer's objection is before using extinguishment. Extinguishment works best on inconsequential issues and with prospects who are not really interested in the salesperson's response.

When to Answer Prospect Objections

Usually the best time to answer a prospect's objection is when it occurs. There are several exceptions to this rule. The salesperson should not counter an objection when:

• The objection will benefit the seller.

- It is obvious that the prospect does not expect an answer.
- The seller is not prepared to answer the objection. However, the seller should explain to the prospect that he or she will respond when they have the information.

The Anatomy of the Sale
Table 3-2
Where Objections Most Commonly Occur During the Five Steps of the Sale

Legend:

Most commonly occur _√√√_
Sometimes occur _√√_
Rarely occur _√_
Never occur _ _

The Five Steps of the Sale	Where Objections Typically Occur
1. Greeting	1. _ _
2. Warm-up	2. _√_
3. Qualification	3. _√√_
4. Presentation	4. _√√√_
5. Close	5. _√√√_

Pitfalls, Causes and Options in Handling Objections

Pitfall #1—Salespeople refuse to accept that prospects have the right to object to or reject whatever they desire. This often causes sellers to botch their replies. This pitfall most often occurs with salespeople who:

- Perceive prospects' objections or rejections as personal affronts.
- Are afraid to deal with such "confrontations."
- Do not respect other people's rights.

These sellers must realize that prospects have the right to object or reject. The salesperson's role is to negotiate a deal that is in the best interest of both parties. To do this, both the salesperson and the prospect must speak freely. Those who take business objections and rejections personally should seek to understand why, so they can remedy this dysfunctional behavior.

Pitfall #2—In dealing with objections, salespeople sometimes overreact and become defensive. Defensive salespeople cause their prospects to react in kind. Defensiveness is caused by insecure sellers who do not feel confident about themselves or their offerings. These sellers typically fail to think out what their prospects want.

More often than not, the prospect's objection is a comment about quality, quantity, or terms of sale. Sellers must realize that the objection is not a personal rejection, but a rejection of some aspect of their offering. To avoid becoming overly emotionally involved in the sale, sellers should understand that prospects are not rejecting them. Before answering prospects, sellers should ask themselves, "What is motivating the prospect to make such a statement. How can I best answer the objection (comment, criticism or question)?"

Prospect rejections and objections are positive, because they indicate that the prospect has been listening to the seller's presentation. The most difficult type of customer to deal with is that individual who does not openly communicate with the salesperson. As long as the customer is communicating, the selling agent has an opportunity to develop a two-way dialogue that will benefit all concerned.

Pitfall #3—Some salespeople believe that objections and rejections are negative, which leads to fear of them. These sellers interpret objections and rejections as the prospect saying "I'm not really interested'" rather than "So far my needs have not been met. What are you going to do to satisfy them so that we might strike a deal here?"

Salespeople must understand that objections and rejection are not necessarily negative. Objections are opportunities for further discussing the customer's needs. When a customer says to a salesperson, "Your delivery schedule doesn't meet our particular needs," this is an opportunity for the salesperson to ask, "Why?"

Why is an important word to the seller. By asking, *Why?*, sellers are encouraging their prospects to clarify their needs. Once they better understand their prospects' needs, salespeople can tailor their presentations to meet them. Also, prospects do not always say what they mean when they raise objections. For instance, when prospects say, "Your price is too high," they may not be objecting to the salesperson's price at all. Rather, they may be saying:

- "You haven't given me a reason to buy."
- "To my knowledge your price doesn't justify the quality of your services."
- "I'm not really prepared to negotiate with you at this time."

Salespeople must learn how to respond to objections and rejections in a positive fashion. Effective techniques for overcoming the fear of dealing with objections and rejection include:

- Arming oneself with a positive attitude.
- Preparing through reading and roleplaying.
- Practicing techniques and responses for handling a prospect's objections and rejection.

The Word No

Many salespeople seem to fear hearing the word *no* from their prospects. They fear this word because they have not analyzed its usage or meaning. The word does not necessarily mean:

- "Never."
- "Not a chance."
- "You have no hope of doing business with me."

Prospects frequently use the word *no* in a variety of ways. It is the salesperson's responsibility to probe the prospect and to uncover what the prospect means by *no*. For example, when a prospect says *no* it can mean:

- "Not at this time."
- "I don't have the power to make this decision."
- "I don't understand (but I don't want to confess this to you)."

The use of the word *no* can be confusing since sometimes it can even mean *yes*.

Chapter Summary

1. A sales *question* helps you gather information or lead a prospect to some conclusion.
2. There are four major sales question groups:
    *   General or open questions.
    *   Reflective or probing questions.
    *   Specific or closed questions.
    *   Leading questions.
3. The skillful use of questions can help you in:
    *   Gaining information necessary for the sale.
    *   Overcoming objections, fears or hidden hostilities.
    *   Validating customer needs.
    *   Planning the right sales strategy.
    *   Making efficient use of time.
    *   Building rapport and understanding.
    *   Leading the prospect to some conclusion.
    *   Creating confidence.
    *   Spreading doubt.
    *   Reconfirming some statement or issue.
    *   Closing the sale.
4. You should ask questions when you want to:
    *   Clarify an issue.
    *   Gather information.
    *   Plant information.
    *   Intimidate a customer.
    *   Guide the listener to a given point.
    *   Draw the customer's attention to some issue.
    *   Test the customer's readiness to make a buying decision.
    *   Box in, or trap, the customer into agreeing with you.
5. An *objection* is any statement the customer gives for rejecting your employer, product, services, ideas or price.

6. Objections can be grouped into six major categories:

    • Intellectual objections.

    • Personal objections.

    • Visceral objections.

    • Imaginary objections.

    • Valid objections.

    • Excuses.

7. Your objectives in handling a prospect's objections are:

    • To help the prospect clarify their objection (if necessary).

    • To identify the cause of a prospect's objection (if not evident).

    • To select ways to handle an objection.

8. When handled well, objections can become selling opportunities.

9. You can respond to an objection in a variety of ways. Here are the *Five Classic Ways to Respond to Customer Objections*:

    • Answer the objection directly with a statement.

    • Answer the objection with a question or series of questions, and then address the objection.

    • Allow the prospects to handle their own objections by asking them leading questions.

    • Extinguish the issue by not responding to the prospect's objection.

    • Agreeing with the prospect.

10. *Qualitative questions* are indirect queries. Usually these questions deal with nontangible information such as feelings, thoughts and emotions.

11. *Qualifying* an objection means encouraging prospects to express their feelings about the objection.

12. *Quantitative questions* are direct queries that call for specific responses. Usually these questions deal with tangible things such as facts, figures, sources, times, places and dates.

13. *Quantifying* an objection means encouraging a customer to give you facts that reveal the reason for the objection.

4

Three Ways
to Romance the Sale,
Customer, Product and Service

*Constructive analysis,
positive thinking, practice and
visualizing one's success are crucial to a
salesperson's competence, confidence and
performance. Salespeople who are competent
and confident (without being arrogant)
will find customers sensing this
and wanting to deal with them.*

After meeting with six different retail computer salespeople, I called one of my acquaintances who sold for a computer manufacturer.

"How's your search for a computer coming along?" he asked.

"Not well," I offered. "It seems as though the people who are capable of answering my technical questions are not sensitive to my needs. In other words the 'techies' don't understand business or people, so it appears impossible for them to answer my nontechnical questions."

"Are you saying that you haven't met many good computer salespeople?"

"Right. That's why I need some advice from someone who understands both computers and my needs. As a result of our earlier conversations I feel that your advice has always been objective and offered in my best interests."

"Has anything significant changed regarding your needs since our last meeting?"

"No."

"Well, I'm not very objective about microcomputers. I feel that we have the best micro on the market."

"But six months ago you told me *not* to buy one of your company's computers," I reminded him.

"Well, six months ago I wasn't certain that this was the real direction our company was going to take."

"So you feel that your company is dedicated to this line of computers?"

"For at least the next five years, it's safe to say we are."

"So what's the value to me?"

His next few statements personalized several important factors to me as he said, "First, you have the confidence of knowing that the product you buy from us will not be phased out of production in a short period. The biggest names in the software business are aware of this as well, and have finally made a commitment to making the software that business people like yourself need."

"But my needs are limited."

"Now they are, but as your company grows, so will your need to process information," he pointed out. He then proceeded to enhance his product's value (a technique called *romancing the product*) by adding, "Just think, you could buy a product that will grow in value to your company. As your business grows, so will your need for the added services this product provides. You're making an investment not only for the present but also for the future."

"That sounds good, but frankly I'm not comfortable with the idea of using a computer."

"You're like many of our other customers. That's why we have radically redesigned our microcomputer—to fit your requests and needs. Too many of our competitors' computers, and too many of our past models, were difficult to use for noncomputer-oriented people. This unit is the most user friendly model available anywhere."

"Everyone claims their computers are user friendly," I complained.

"You're right. Here's the way to discover which of those computers is user friendly—simply use their computers and then test our micro. You'll find the differences between their computers and our micro are amazing. Because of my background, I learned how to use our unit in hours. You'll be happily surprised to see how quickly you will master our word processing package. And remember, as you described, your greatest immediate needs revolve around a simple yet professional word processing package. We've got it, and you can have it too, once you're using one of our models."

"Is it really that easy to learn?"

"Exceptionally easy. But don't take my word for it—test one of our units," he urged. Before I could say another word he began comparing (a technique called *pairing*) his product to successful images, further enhancing his computer's image. "We're quickly becoming the Rolls Royce of our industry. The best part of it all is that we're delivering Rolls Royce quality at a BMW price."

"Sounds good," I said with a chuckle.

"Almost too good, except that it's all true," he assured me. Then he began encouraging me to see myself using his product and feeling successful in the process (a technique called *placing the customer in the picture of success*) by saying, "Listen, our micro is so easy to use that you'll soon be using it with little or no effort. You'll access information, draft letters, produce reports and find data without bothering your secretary. Your secretary's time is valuable, and you also could save yourself the time it takes to explain what it is you're looking for. In the time it takes to explain to your people what you want, you can access it yourself, quickly and easily."

"It sounds like you're trying to sell me a computer," I teased.

"No, I'm just trying to help you make the wisest choice for your present and future needs," he replied. "Let me schedule an appointment for you with one of our best retailers in the area. They're honest people, provide good service and will support you with the technical information you need as you learn how to use your micro. Is Thursday or Friday a better day for you?"

"Friday," I answered.

"I'll set up the appointment with them and verify their availability with you tomorrow."

My friend is an excellent salesperson. Knowing that I was uncomfortable with using a computer, he used the term *computer* sparingly. He referred to his competition's products as *computers* and his company's computers as *units* and *micros*. He did not ask me questions regarding my needs during this discussion because he had done so during our earlier meetings. But he was wise in asking me if my needs had changed since our last meeting. Once I answered him, he was free to make his comments.

He employed a number of professional selling techniques very effectively. Three of those techniques were purposely pointed out in the preceding copy. Those three subjects are also the main topics of this chapter:

Pairing

Romancing the Sale

Placing the Customer in the Picture of Success

At first glance these three topics may appear to be the same technique, but each differs from the others in some very subtle ways. There is some overlap in purpose and practice. Still, a seller has to be careful in introducing and using these techniques.

Evaluating Your Understanding of the Cornerstones of Selling

Part III—Pairing, Romancing the Sale, and Placing the Customer in the Picture of Success

Before reading further you may desire to examine your awareness of these three subjects. For that reason we have included a self-assessment exercise here. If you have not read the instructions that precede the self-assessment exercise in Chapter 2, page 17, you might review them at this time. These sections are titled *Evaluating Your Understanding of the Cornerstones of Selling* and *Exercise Suggestions*.

Exercise

Cornerstones of Selling Study
Part III—Pairing, Romancing the Sale,
and Placing the Customer in the Picture of Success

Instructions:

Check the letter next to the answer that is most accurate. Please mark only one selection for each question. For example:

0.	I like to sell to:
	a. New prospects.
	b. People I know.
√	c. It doesn't matter.

In making your selections:

- Do not mark any phrase you are uncertain of or that does not apply.

- Check the *Glossary* or *Index* for any word that is unfamiliar.

- Be as honest as possible, and mark the way you actually perform or behave.

This is a continuation of the Cornerstones of Selling Study Exercise.
This section begins with number 61.

61. *Placing the customer in the picture of success* means to:

    a. Show him or her a picture of the offering.

    b. Help the prospects visualize their satisfaction with their purchase.

    c. Neither of the above.

62. I help buyers visualize satisfaction with their purchase:

    a. Yes, I employ this technique regularly.

    b. I rarely, if ever, use this technique.

    c. I use this technique when I think of it.

63. Prospects are more likely to buy when they:

    a. Are pressured to make a purchase.

    b. Have run out of objections.

    c. Feel their purchases will satisfy their needs.

64. My prospects would rate my ability to implement placing the customer in the picture of success:

    a. As excellent.

    b. As average.

    c. I do not use this selling technique.

65. I know what images appeal to my prospects:

    a. Yes.

    b. No.

    c. I occasionally evaluate what images are most appealing.

66. One instance in which I will use placing the customer in the picture of success is when the:

    a. Prospect is getting ready to end our meeting.

    b. Prospects cannot see themselves using what I am selling.

    c. I do not use this selling technique.

67. Which sentence is an example of placing the customer in the picture of success statement?

    a. "Using this vitamin means you are using the best."

    b. "Using this vitamin will make you healthier and stronger."

    c. "Using this vitamin will change your present condition, I'm sure."

68. Which statement is an example of a placing the customer in the picture of success?

    a. "When you use this spa you'll thank me."

    b. "When you use this spa you'll be the 1,000th customer to do so."

    c. "When you use this spa you'll feel warm and relaxed."

69. Which statement is an example of using subtleness to place the customer in the picture of success?

    a. "These apples are the reddest you'll find in the market."

    b. "These apples are sweet, crisp, cold and juicy."

    c. "These apples are the only ones grown locally."

70. Which statement is an example of overtly placing the customer in the picture of success?

    a. "Imagine sleeping in this bed and feeling relaxed in it right now."

    b. "This is the firmest mattress available anywhere."

    c. "This bed is guaranteed to be comfortable."

71. Citing similarities between an employer, products and services and a successful image is called:

    a. Placing the customer in the picture of success.

    b. Pairing.

    c. Romancing the sale.

72. I pair my employer, products, and services, with other successful vendors and their products, and services:

    a. Yes.

    b. Occasionally.

    c. I rarely, if ever, use pairing.

73. The purpose of pairing is:

    a. To brag about my employer, products, and services.

    b. To enhance the image of my employer, products, and services.

    c. I don't know.

74. An effective way to use the pairing process:

    a. Is to be overt (obvious) about my employer, products, and services.

    b. Is to be subtle (low-key) about my employer, products and services.

    c. Will vary from selling situation to selling situation.

75. I know what pairing images appeal to my prospects:

    a. Yes.

    b. No.

    c. I do not use this selling technique.

76. My prospects would rate my pairing abilities as:

    a. Excellent.

    b. Fair.

    c. I do not use this selling technique.

77. I can use a variety of pairing examples comfortably and at will:

    a. Yes.

    b. No.

    c. I do not use this selling technique.

78. Which sentence is an example of a pairing statement?

    a. "We are a financially secure organization."

    b. "We are as financially secure as anyone."

    c. "We are as financially secure as the strongest vendors."

79. Which sentence is an example of a pairing statement?

    a. "Like the other smart business leaders, we are innovative."

    b. "We are a very innovative organization."

    c. "Innovation is important to us."

80. Which sentence is an example of a pairing statement?

    a. "Our company is number one."

    b. "We consider ourselves to be the best vendor here."

    c. "As the QE-II model was the best in her time, we are tops now."

81. Saying positive things about one's employer, products and services is called:

    a. Placing the customer in the picture of success.

    b. Pairing.

    c. Romancing the sale.

82. I make positive statements about my employer, products and services:
    a. As often as possible when it is appropriate to do so.
    b. Occasionally.
    c. Rarely, if ever.

83. The purpose in saying positive things about my employer, products, and services is to:
    a. Get my prospect to think in positive terms about them.
    b. Knock the competition.
    c. Pretend that I like them.

84. An effective way to use the romancing the sale process:
    a. Is to be overt (obvious) about my employer, products, and services.
    b. Is to be subtle (low-key) about my employer, products, and services.
    c. Is to skip this technique.

85. I know what romancing images appeal to my prospects:
    a. Yes.
    b. No.
    c. I do not use this selling technique.

86. My prospects would rate my romancing the sale abilities as:
    a. Excellent.
    b. Fair.
    c. I do not use this selling technique.

87. I am most likely to use the romancing the sale process:
    a. When I want to flaunt the success of my employer, products, and services.
    b. When I want to enhance the image of my employer, products, and services.
    c. I do not use this selling technique.

88. Which statement is an example of *romancing the sale*?

    a. "Fashion models use our brand because it's inexpensive."

    b. "Fashion models use our brand because it's well-known."

    c. "Fashion models use our brand because it enhances their beauty."

89. Which statement is an example of *romancing the sale*?

    a. "We are rated as the top vendor by industry buyers."

    b. "We are rated as the top vendor by our customers."

    c. "We consider ourselves to be the top vendor in the area."

90. Which statement is an example of *romancing the sale*?

    a. "Our services are used by many hotels."

    b. "Our services are used by the hotel industry."

    c. "Our services are used by the best hotels in the world."

Scoring

Cornerstones of Selling Study
Part III—Pairing, Romancing the Sale,
and Placing the Customer in the Picture of Success

Legend:

PRG — Pairing.

RTS — Romancing the Sale.

PCPs — Placing the Customer in the Picture of Success.

Instructions:

From the previous *Exercise*, circle the same letters below, including the score. After completing this section, proceed to the *Score Box*. Make certain your answers reflect the way you actually interact with your prospects and customers.

---

61. Placing the customer in the picture of success means to:

   a.   0

   b. 10   PCPS

   c.   0

62. I help buyers visualize satisfaction with their purchase:

   a. 10   PCPS

   b.   0

   c.   5   PCPS

63. Prospects are more likely to buy when they:

   a.   0

   b.   0

   c. 10   PCPS

64. My prospects would rate my ability to implement placing the customer in the picture of success:

    a. 10 PCPS

    b. 5 PCPS

    c. 0

65. I know what images appeal to my prospects:

    a. 10 PCPS

    b. 0

    c. 5 PCPS

66. One instance in which I will use placing the customer in the picture of success is when the:

    a. 0

    b. 10 PCPS

    c. 0

67. Which statement is an example of placing the customer in the picture?

    a. 0

    b. 10 PCPS

    c. 0

68. Which statement is an example of placing the customer in the picture?

    a. 0

    b. 0

    c. 10 PCPS

69. Which statement is an example of using subtleness to place the customer in the picture of success?

    a. 0

    b. 10 PCPS

    c. 0

70. Which statement is an example of overtly placing the customer in the picture of success?

    a. 10 PCPS

    b. 0

    c. 0

71. Citing similarities between an employer, products and services and a successful image is called:

    a. 0

    b. 10 PRG

    c. 0

72. I pair my employer, products, and services, with other successful vendors and their products, and services:

    a. 10 PRG

    b. 5 PRG

    c. 0

73. The purpose of pairing my employer, products, and services and other successful employers, products, and services is:

    a. 0

    b. 10 PRG

    c. 0

74. An effective way to use the pairing process:

    a. 5 PRG

    b. 10 PRG

    c. 10 PRG

75. I know what pairing images appeal to my prospects:

    a. 10 PRG

    b. 0

    c. 0

76. My prospects would rate my pairing abilities as:

    a. 10   PRG

    b.   5   PRG

    c.   0

77. I can use a variety of pairing examples comfortably and at will:

    a. 10   PRG

    b.   0

    c.   0

78. Which sentence is an example of a pairing statement?

    a.   0

    b.   0

    c. 10   PRG

79. Which sentence is an example of a pairing statement?

    a. 10   PRG

    b.   0

    c.   0

80. Which sentence is an example of a pairing statement?

    a.   0

    b.   0

    c. 10   PRG

81. Saying positive things about one's employer, products and services is called:

    a.   0

    b.   0

    c. 10   RTS

82. I make positive statements about my employer, products, and services:

    a. 10   RTS

    b.   5   RTS

    c.   0

83. The purpose of saying positive things about my employer, products, and services is to:

    a. 10 RTS

    b. 0

    c. 0

84. An effective way to use the romancing the sale process:

    a. 5 RTS

    b. 10 RTS

    c. 0

85. I know what romancing images appeal to my prospects:

    a. 10 RTS

    b. 0

    c. 0

86. My prospects would rate my romancing the sale abilities as:

    a. 10 RTS

    b. 5 RTS

    c. 0

87. When I use the romancing the sale process I am most likely to use it:

    a. 0

    b. 10 RTS

    c. 0

88. Which statement is an example of romancing the sale?

    a. 0

    b. 0

    c. 10 RTS

89. Which statement is an example of romancing the sale?

    a. 10 RTS

    b. 5 RTS

    c. 0

90. Which statement is an example of an romancing the sale?

    a.   5   RTS

    b.   5   RTS

    c. 10   RTS

Score Box
Cornerstones of Selling Study
Part III—Pairing, Romancing the Sale,
and Placing the Customer in the Picture of Success
Instructions:

Total your score for each category and place it on the line to the right of the appropriate classification:

	Subelement	Total Points
PRG —	Pairing	_____
RTS —	Romancing the Sale	_____
PCPS —	Placing the Customer in	_____
	the Picture of Success	

Find your scores for each category (PCPS, PRG, RTS) on the following page. If your total score for any category is 80, 70, or 60, read both phrases (just above and below that score). The following analysis is based on the accuracy of your selections. It reviews only the technical aspects of your selling practices.

If your responses are correct and a reflection of your actual selling performance, the following assessment will be accurate. Other critical factors that impact your selling success (for example: appearance, body language, confidence, voice, product or service knowledge, and subelements of the sale) are not factored into this study.

Awareness Level and Probable Tendencies
Cornerstones of Selling Study
Part III — Pairing, Romancing the Sale, and Placing the Customer in the Picture of Success

PCPS	PRG	RTS
80 – 100 Points		
You are able to place the customer in the picture of success with ease. You should be extremely good at using the PCPS process.	To you pairing is a simple selling skill. You are probably effective in using it subtly.	Romancing the sale is easy for you to use. You know it is an effective tool and you use it in both professional and personal matters.
70 – 80 Points		
You are aware of prospects' needs to see themselves as satisfied with their purchases. Using PCPS shows that you are sensitive to your prospects.	You are aware of the importance of pairing. Use it consistently and your sales will improve.	You are sensitive to your prospects' needs and may use this skill when it suits your purposes.
60 – 70 Points		
Spend more time thinking like a customer and you will find yourself using this technique more often and more successfully.	You use pairing occasionally. This hit-or-miss approach may be costing you sales.	Where you have a high interest in the sale or prospect, you may use romancing the sale well. Otherwise you tend to abandon it.

If you scored 60 points or lower in any of these categories:

a.   Increase your knowledge of the subelement in question.

b.   Practice using the subelement in front of a mirror or with others.

c.   Video tape your roleplays and allow a qualified person to critique you.

Regardless of how well you scored, review the practices recommended in this chapter. Look for those techniques that can help you, and put them to work as soon as possible.

Placing the Customer
in the Picture of Success

Placing the customer in the picture of success is also known as *PCPS* and *the picture of success*. It is an old selling technique salespeople use to influence the way a prospect views the seller, products, and services. PCPS is not a selling tool every salesperson can use well. Sellers who lack confidence may find it more difficult to use than those who believe in themselves and in their products and services. Once mastered, PCPS is easy to initiate. It is effective because:

- Interested prospects want to know what they will derive from their purchase.
- Prospects who like the sellers are usually looking for reasons to buy from them, and PCPS can help the prospects through that process.

Definition of PCPS

Placing the customer in the picture of success occurs when the seller helps the customer visualize and mentally or emotionally experience the benefits he or she will derive from using the product or service.

Purpose and Objectives of PCPS

Prospects may feel uneasy with unfamiliar products, services, vendors and salespeople. This uneasiness makes the selling process more difficult for both buyer and seller. The purpose of PCPS is to help the prospect become more comfortable with the salesperson, product and service.

The objectives of the PCPS technique are to:

- Encourage prospects to lower their defenses.
- Help prospects develop a sense of ownership of the sellers' products and services.
- Help prospects visualize their own success as a direct result of using the seller's products or services.
- Influence prospects to feel more favorable toward the use and purchase of a seller's products or services.

Types of PCPS Presentations

There are two general types of PCPS classifications—*subtle* and *overt*. The more sophisticated the prospect, the more subtle the use of the PCPS process must be. The less sophisticated the customer, the more overt the PCPS example. Here are two versions:

1. An example of *subtle PCPS*—Seller (referring to a picture of a chair): "Nothing feels as good to the body as a well-contoured chair like this one. It's ergonomically designed to offer you the kind of comfort, support and utility you're looking for in a chair."

2. An example of *overt PCPS*—Seller (referring to a picture of a chair): "Imagine yourself sitting in this wonderful chair. Your muscles relax as your spine rests comfortably in the padded back. Sitting in this piece of art for long periods of time will seem like minutes. It is designed for maximum comfort and support. You can move and reach things rapidly and easily, as the ergonomic design feels custom-tailored to your body."

How to Implement PCPS

The easiest way for sellers to initiate the PCPS process is to encourage prospects to imagine successfully using the product or service. Salespeople should then explain to the prospects how and what they will enjoy as a result of using their products or services. Here is an example:

Initiating the PCPS in Business-to-Business Sales	Initiating the PCPS in Consumer Sales
"Just imagine how impressed your boss and peers will be when they see how much money you're saving your organization through this purchase."	"Just imagine our cool mint chocolate ice cream slowly melting on your tongue, pleasantly quenching your thirst. Yes, it's creamy, rich, cool, wet and perfectly sweetened. You can taste it right now, can't you? Sure is good."

Initiating the PCPS Technique

There are several times during the sale when you can initiate the PCPS process:
- During the presentation step.
- Just before a closing statement.
- When you need to gain or recapture waning customer attention.

The Anatomy of the Sale
Table 4-1
Initiating PCPS in the Five Steps of the Sale

Legend:

Excellent step to initiate $\_\sqrt{}\sqrt{}\sqrt{}\_$
Good step to initiate $\_\sqrt{}\sqrt{}\_$
Fair step to initiate $\_\sqrt{}\_$
Poor step to initiate$\_ \_$

The Five Steps of the Sale	Where To Initiate PCPS
1. Greeting	1. $\_ \_$
2. Warm-up	2. $\_ \_$
3. Qualification	3. $\_\sqrt{}\_$
4. Presentation	4. $\_\sqrt{}\sqrt{}\sqrt{}\_$
5. Close	5. $\_\sqrt{}\sqrt{}\_$

PCPS Pitfalls, Causes and Options

Here are a few examples of the kinds of pitfalls salespeople encounter in implementing PCPS:

Pitfall #1—Sellers fail to implement the PCPS technique. Failure to initiate PCPS may be caused by lack of forethought or training. These salespeople should develop a list of phrases that will assist them in initiating the PCPS process. They should discipline themselves to use a PCPS during every selling situation. Furthermore, they should not limit themselves to using only one

PCPS, but vary the number and frequency of PCPSs they use according to the selling circumstances.

Pitfall #2—PCPS may fail because sellers focus attention in areas or on benefits that are not of interest to their prospects. This causes the prospects to feel that the sellers are not interested in them. Often this will kill the sale.

This frequently occurs when the sellers are not paying attention to their customers. Paying more careful attention to their prospect's interests will help sellers avoid these pitfalls.

Pairing

What prospects think of products or services is directly related to what their sellers think of those products and services and how they present them. Pairing is a selling technique that helps salespeople present their products and services in the best possible light. The pairing technique can be extremely helpful in impressing a prospect or shoring up a prospect's image of the salesperson's company, product or service. Its frequent and subtle use makes it a potent selling technique.

Definition of Pairing

Pairing is the act of allying the vendor's reputation, product quality, customer support programs, etc. to that of another successful organization which the customer holds in high regard.

Purpose and Objectives of the Pairing Technique

The purpose of pairing is to help sellers present a positive impression of what they are selling. Through the pairing process, the sellers' objectives are to:
- Enhance their products' and services' images.
- Develop a positive flow to their sales presentations.
- Win their prospects approval of their products and services.

Pairing Types

Pairing falls into several categories, such as:
- Pairing the value of price, guarantees and warranties with others.

- Pairing the quality of product and service with those from other companies.
- Pairing the organization's good reputation to that of other outstanding groups.
- Pairing the quality, efficiency, or speed of delivery with recognized leading companies.

How to Initiate the Pairing Process

Here are some ways to initiate the pairing technique:

Initiating the Pairing Process in Business-to-Business Sales	Initiating the Pairing Process in Consumer Sales
An example of pairing the quality of product and service with other companies of high quality—	
• "As you know, our products are the Rolls Royce of the industry."	• "As you know, our services are the Rolls Royce of the industry."
An example of pairing the importance of product and service quality with consistency and reliability—	
• "Our quality is as consistent and reliable as the rising of the sun."	• "Our quality is as consistent and reliable as the rising of the sun."
An example of pairing quality, efficiency or speed of delivery with recognized leading companies—	
• "Our same-day business courier service makes us the Federal Express of our industry."	• "Our same-day consumer courier service makes us the Federal Express of our industry."
An example of pairing an organization's good reputation to other outstanding groups—	
• "Like the quality leaders of any business-sensitive company, we keep attracting new accounts. The secret is our after-sales support of our clients."	• "Like the quality leaders of any consumer-sensitive company, we keep attracting new customers. The secret is our after-sales support of our customers."

Continued on next page.

Initiating the Pairing Process in Business-to-Business Sales	Initiating the Pairing Process in Consumer Sales
An example of pairing an organization's financial standing to other groups— • "Our company is a medium-sized supplier to your industry. Yet, we are more financially stable than the world's top 100 companies."	• "Our company is medium-sized. Financially speaking, we are the most stable group selling directly to consumers."

Initiating the Pairing Process

The time for salespeople to use pairing examples is when they sense that it is important to enhance their image regarding their employer, product, service, or terms of sale.

The Anatomy of the Sale
Table 4-2
Initiating Pairing in the Five Steps of the Sale

Legend:
Excellent step to initiate _√√√_
Good step to initiate _√√_
Fair step to initiate _√_
Poor step to initiate_ _

The Five Steps of the Sale	Where To Initiate the Pairing Process
1. Greeting	1. _ _
2. Warm-up	2. _ _
3. Qualification	3. _√√√_
4. Presentation	4. _√√√_
5. Close	5. _√√_

Pairing Pitfalls, Causes and Options

Here are a few examples of the kinds of pitfalls sellers encounter in using pairing:

Pitfall #1—Sellers fail to use good or relevant pairing examples. Usually, they are not paying attention to their prospect's need for such references.

Pitfall #2—Salespeople use a pairing example at the wrong time. These people are not aware of the importance of timing in using the pairing process. To avoid this pitfall, these sellers should write out, practice and consciously use pairing examples in roleplaying situations and in their sales calls.

Pitfall #3—Sellers fail to prequalify prospects' awareness and opinions of the third party before using that party as a reference. This mistake occurs when salespeople are not paying attention to their sales presentation or are not interested in the prospect. This challenge can be overcome:

- With a change of attitude.
- By taking a listening course.
- Through counseling with someone who is sensitive to this problem.

Romancing the Sale

Romancing the sale is also known as *romancing the product*, *romancing the service*, or simply *romancing*. It is a technique that sellers use to enhance the image of their products, services, prices or companies. An easy technique to master, it is most effective when the sellers believe in what they are presenting. If the sellers do not believe in what they are saying, the entire process will backfire. Romancing the sale is similar to the technique of placing the customer in the picture of success.

Definition of Romancing the Sale

Romancing the Sale is the process of making the product or service, or the customer's use of it, appear positive.

Purpose and Objectives of Romancing the Sale

The purpose of the romancing process is to help the prospect think of the seller's company, product, service or price more favorably. The salesperson's objectives in the romancing process are to:

- Cast something or someone in a romantic, positive or favorable light.
- Minimize the negative effects of other issues (for example; high price, poor past relations, lack of quality or poor service).
- Help prospects visualize their becoming happier, healthier, more successful or better as a result of using the seller's products and services (see *Placing the Customer in the Picture of Success.*)

Types of Romancing Processes

There are two romancing classifications—*subtle* and *overt*.

How To Implement the Romancing Process

One way of romancing some aspect of the sale is for the seller to begin by talking about the issue's value to the prospect and specifically how that prospect will benefit from its purchase. The salesperson must modify the romancing technique to fit the situation and the prospect's personality. The more sophisticated the customer, the more subtle the romancing effort should be. The less sophisticated the buyer, the more overt the romancing effort should be.

Initiating the Romancing Process in Business-to-Business Sales	Initiating the Romancing Process in Consumer Sales
An example of romancing the product or service—	
• "The top three manufacturers in your industry use our products."	• "The most fashionable consumers are wearing our clothes this season."

Initiating the Romancing Process in Business-to-Business or Consumer Sales	
An example of romancing the seller's company— "Once a prospect becomes our customer we keep that customer because of our product and service quality. We know this because nine out of every ten sales we make are to repeat customers."	
An example of romancing the seller's price— "This is the lowest price for the highest quality service available anywhere. Just think of what you can enjoy with your savings."	

Initiating the Romancing Process

The romancing process often appears during two extremely different situations:
- When the prospect does not like the product, service, vendor or seller.
    or
- When the customer likes the product, service, vendor and salesperson and is looking for a reason to buy.

The Anatomy of the Sale
Table 4-3
Initiating the Romancing Process in the Five Steps of the Sale

Legend:

Excellent step to initiate _√√√_
Good step to initiate _√√_
Fair step to initiate _√_
Poor step to initiate_ _

The Five Steps of the Sale	Where To Initiate the Romancing Process
1. Greeting	1. _ _
2. Warm-up	2. _ _
3. Qualification	3. _√_
4. Presentation	4. _√√√_
5. Close	5. _√√_

Romancing the Sale Pitfalls, Causes and Options

Here are a few examples of the kinds of pitfalls sellers encounter in using the romancing process:

Pitfall #1—Salespeople who skip the romancing the sale technique. This can result from lack of training in implementing the romancing the sale process. As in other subelements of the sale, these sellers should develop a written list of romancing the sale statements and then discipline themselves to use a *romancing the sale* during every selling situation.

Pitfall #2—Sellers who are overly subtle with unsophisticated prospects or are too overt with sophisticated customers, can create misunderstandings and impaired communication. Occasionally, sellers begin their sales presentations without considering their prospect's personality needs. They fail to identify the most effective and appropriate tactic for communicating with the customer, persuading and employing the romancing the sale technique.

Before and during the selling process, salespeople should examine their prospects' interests and basic personality tendencies (behavior and likely reactions). After they understand both, they should plan their selling approach and their usage of the romancing the sale technique.

Chapter Summary

1. *Placing the customer in the picture of success* occurs when you help prospects visualize and mentally experience the benefits they will derive from using your products or services.
2. You should implement the *PCPS* technique when you want to:
    *   Encourage prospects to lower their defenses.
    *   Help prospects develop a sense of ownership of your products and services.
    *   Influence prospects to feel more favorable toward the use and purchase of your products or services.
    *   Help prospects visualize that they will achieve greater success as a direct result of using your products or services.
3. There are two general types of *PCPS* classifications-*subtle* and *overt*.
4. The easiest way for you to initiate the *PCPS* process is to encourage customers to imagine using your product or service successfully. You should then explain to them what they will experience and how much they will enjoy it as a result of using your product or service.
5. There are several times during the sale that you should initiate the *PCPS* process:
    *   During the presentation step.
    *   Just before a closing statement.
    *   When you need to gain or recapture waning customer attention.
6. *Pairing* is the act of allying your company's reputation, quality of products, services, guarantees, warranties, price, customer support programs, delivery time or other business conduct to that of a successful organization that the customer holds in high regard.
7. *Pairing* falls into several categories, such as:
    *   Pairing the quality of product and service with the high quality of that from other companies.
    *   Pairing the value of price, guarantees and warranties with others of high value.
    *   Pairing the quality, efficiency, or speed of delivery with recognized leading companies.

- Pairing the organization's good reputation with that of other outstanding groups.
8. The time for you to use a *pairing* example is when you sense that it is important to enhance the image of your company's reputation, product, service, guarantee, warranty, price, customer support program or delivery time.
9. *Romancing the sale* makes the customers' use of the product or service sound exceptionally positive.
10. Your objectives in the *romancing* process are to:
    - Cast something or someone in a romantic, positive or favorable light.
    - Minimize the negative effects of other issues (for example, high price, poor past relations, lack of quality or poor service).
    - Help prospects to visualize becoming happier, healthier, more successful or better as a result of using your products and services.
11. One way of *romancing* some aspect of the sale is to begin by talking about the issue's value to the prospect and specifically how that buyer will benefit from its purchase.
12. You should implement *romancing* when:
    - Prospects don't like your product, service, or employer.
    - Prospects indicate that they are looking for a reason to buy from you.

5

The Little
Sales Techniques That
Make a Big Difference in Selling

*Nobody
wants to be
sold to. Nobody
wants to be sold
at. Avoid pressuring
yourself to make a sale.
Avoid pressuring your customers
to make a purchase. Forcing people to bend
to your desires only creates ill will. Instead, before
making your next sales call, tell yourself:* The sale is
complete. I am here merely to arrange the details.

The two representatives from the computer store entered my office. I recognized them immediately for they had recently attended one of our company's sales and marketing management courses.

After we exchanged greetings and a few social pleasantries, the sales manager began by saying, "I asked our store manager to accompany me today. He can address the technical questions that I may not be able to answer."

Smart, I thought. *These people feel that I'm important enough to send their store manager along with their sales manager to talk with me. And I like their approach. A good sales technique.*

It soon became evident that their selling strategy was both professional and effective. They were thorough in evaluating my present needs and discussed future needs as well. They also confirmed information they had gathered the day before during a telephone conversation with me.

The sales manager then said, "We represent fourteen different systems suitable for companies such as yours. So we had to narrow that number to the best five models. Because of the last few things you mentioned to us today, I'd like to revise our recommendations to these two systems."

With that he handed me two pamphlets describing two very different computer systems and turned to his associate and asked, "How do you feel about my recommendations?"

The store manager looked at me and said, "Since you and your employees aren't computer literate, I'd have to agree that these two systems are the easiest to learn of the fourteen we offer. But please look at all five systems. You should understand what your options are."

"I'm already somewhat familiar with most of these systems," I mentioned.

"Then let's look at the differences," the sales manager replied.

"Good," I said.

Both of them then outlined the differences between machines, taking great care in pointing out what these variations would mean to me.

Impressed with their presentation, I said, "Yesterday I mentioned that I was also considering another computer that you don't handle. It also seems to have many options I need for my business."

"It's a good computer," the store manager agreed.

The sales manager chimed in, "It *is* good. Did the salesperson at the other store bother to explain all the features to you?"

"Whatever he could explain in the hour I spent with him," I answered.

"Excellent," the sales manager replied. "Then he explained the time needed to learn his system."

"No, he didn't," I said.

Here it comes, I thought. *Now he's going to explain the differences between his best computer and the competition's. Let's see if he does this tactfully.*

The sales manager suggested, "For the sake of brevity, let me explain the differences between their product and this model. If ease of use and quick learning time is important to you, then this is the machine for you and your company. In the years to come you'll save thousands of dollars and hundreds of hours training new staff members on this computer as opposed to the other one you mentioned. The reason is that it takes 35 percent less time for a noncomputer-oriented person to learn how to use this machine as opposed to the other one. I believe the time saved is more like 45 to 50 percent, but the 35 percent figure comes from a microcomputer school here in the city. If you'd like to phone them and verify their experiences with the two machines, I'll be happy to give you their number."

What a professional approach to the differences in the training time between his computer and the competition's, I thought. *The sales manager's method of quoting a third party's estimates is important and highly effective.*

The store manager then offered, "They not only like the machine, they also plan to buy more of these units. They plan to buy more of them because of *(1)* the ease of teaching computer skills on this model, *(2)* the short training time involved and *(3)* their feeling that the business market is going to turn to micros more and more."

Their enthusiastic comments are contributing to the selling process nicely. They are scoring well against their competition in a highly positive way.

"And this new model is going to be one of the leaders because of its advanced approach to microcomputing," the sales manager added.

"Yes, I'd like to talk with the computer school people," I replied.

The store manager suggested, "Ask them about the differences in the features, software and users' attitudes toward both as well."

The other manager quickly added, "They will most likely explain that this unit's weakness is that the software available at this time is limited. That's an accurate statement, but according to several computer magazines, 200 new programs for this computer are going to hit the market within the next 60 days. You can read this news for yourself in the two magazines I've brought with me. Even if it takes a few more months for the software to come to market, it won't affect you. Your immediate needs are for word processing and an accounting package. These types of programs are already available, with more on the way. So no matter how many other kinds of programs other models have available, none of them will be of use to you right now."

I like the way he took his product's weakness of limited software availability and neutralized it. He was also extremely effective in the way he diminished the competition's strength in the many programs they have available. He did all this without a derogatory or negative statement about his competition.

"You're right about my immediate software needs," I stated. "But my greatest concern is training and technical support."

"I'm glad you brought that up," the sales manager stated assertively.

This person is really positive. He doesn't back away from any challenge. It sounds like he was waiting for me to mention training and technical support.

"There are larger computer retailers in this town with larger staffs," he continued. "But no one is going to take the personal interest in your needs and business that we do. That's why both of us came to see you today. To us, you don't represent just the sale of a computer, you represent a continuing future relationship. I'll come to your office personally and spend a couple of hours explaining the use of our machine when you receive it. If you decide to purchase one today, I'll deliver it myself Monday afternoon and review its capabilities with you then. That way you can start using it immediately. Later you can come to our store for formal training."

I like that kind of personalized service.

"And if you have a problem, just call me or one of my assistants," the store manager suggested. "There's no charge for the time we spend training you in your office for that first session. There is a charge for the formal training in our store, but the follow-up advice you may need, and requests by telephone will come at no charge. We recently surveyed our competitors and found that they usually offer one or two of these services but not all three. Sooner or later they will catch up with us. But people like you need these services now! You're not just buying a computer, you're also buying a computer company."

Good point. How clever of him to begin stressing the differences between his retailing organization and others.

"Most of our competitors are small businesses that send their computers to other locations for repair," the sales manager said. "This too is changing and most are trying to do repair work within their stores, as we do. Keep in mind the time you might lose dealing with a retailer who has to send your computer elsewhere for work. Then figure how much time and money you can save dealing with our company that has an in-house technical support department."

He covered another difference that's important to me and stated it extremely well. They have just made a sale. I hope they can live up to their commitments. (They did.)

The two managers continued pointing out the differences between their product and the competition's. They were fair and quickly pointed out where the competition was stronger and noted what their machine could do to compensate for its weakness. Their approach was effective because they were able to *stress the differences* (known as the *STD* process) between themselves and the competition in a genuinely positive and professional fashion. This approach was so effective that they did not have to ask or make a closing statement, as I made the closing statement before they asked for my business.

This chapter addresses the STD process that the two managers employed so effectively. It also includes sections on *transitional phrases*, *what to do after the sale is closed* and *the importance of developing a positive sales presentation.*

Evaluating Your Understanding of the Cornerstones of Selling

Part IV—Transitional Phrases and Stressing the Difference

Before reading further you may want to examine your awareness of these two subjects. For that reason we have included a self-assessment exercise here. If you have not read the instructions that precede the self-assessment exercise in Chapter 2 you might review them at this time. These sections are titled *Evaluating Your Understanding of the Cornerstones of Selling* and *Exercise Suggestions*.

Exercise
Cornerstones of Selling Study
Part IV—Transitional
Phrases and Stressing the Difference

Instructions:

Check the letter next to the answer that is most accurate. Please mark only one selection for each question. For example:

```
      0.    I like to sell to:
            a.  New prospects.
            b.  People I know.
      √     c.  It doesn't matter.
```

In making your selections:

- Do not mark any phrase you are uncertain of or that does not apply.
- Check the *Glossary* or *Index* for any word that is unfamiliar.
- Be as honest as possible, and mark the way you actually perform or behave.

This is a continuation of the Cornerstones of Selling Study Exercise.
This section begins with number 91.

91. Stressing the difference means emphasizing the difference between:

    a. My qualification and problem solving efforts.

    b. My employer, products and services and the competition's employer, products and services.

    c. Neither of the above.

92. My purpose in using the stressing the difference process is to:

    a. Give me the opportunity to talk with the prospect.

    b. Give prospects an understanding of differences between my employer, products and services and the competition's employer, products and services

    c. I do not use this selling technique.

93. I point out the differences between my employer, products and services and the competition's employer, products and services:

    a. As positively as possible and whenever it's appropriate.

    b. Occasionally.

    c. Never.

94. My prospects would rate my ability to implement the *stressing the difference* process:

    a. As excellent.

    b. As average.

    c. I do not use this selling technique.

95. I know what *stressing the difference* phrases appeal or are acceptable to my prospects:

    a. Yes.

    b. No.

    c. I have never evaluated this process.

96. I am most likely to use *stressing the difference* when:

    a. The prospect has agreed to purchase my products or services.

    b. The prospect is trying to evaluate my employer, products and services against the competition's employer, products, and services.

    c. I do not use this selling technique.

97. When I do stress the differences between my employer, products, and services and the competition's employer, products, and services:

    a. I do so in an overt or obvious fashion.

    b. I do so in a subtle or low-key fashion.

    c. I do not use this selling technique.

98. I can cite the differences between my employer, products and services and the competition's employer, products and services easily:

    a. Yes.

    b. No.

    c. I do not use this selling technique.

99. Which phrase is an example of a *stressing the difference* statement?

    a. "We offer you more and at a lower price than our competitors do."

    b. "We offer a large quantity at a low price with an extended guarantee."

    c. "We offer you a discount price for quantity purchases, as well as a guarantee."

100. Which phrase is an example of a *stressing the difference* statement?

    a. "Our guarantee is all encompassing."

    b. "Our guarantee covers lots of things you probably never expected."

    c. "Unlike your supplier, our guarantee covers both labor and parts."

101. A transitional phrase is a phrase that helps a seller:

    a. Move from one step of the sale (or from one idea) to another.

    b. Explain his or her move from one employer to another.

    c. Neither of the above.

102. An effective use of a transitional phrase:

    a. Is overt (obvious).

    b. Is subtle (low-key).

    c. Will vary from sale to sale.

103. I know what transitional phrase's are effective for my selling style:

    a. Yes.

    b. No.

    c. I do not use this selling technique.

104. My prospect would rate my ability to move smoothly from idea to idea as:

    a. Excellent.

    b. Average.

    c. Below average.

105. I can use a variety of transitional phrase's comfortably and whenever I desire:

    a. Yes.

    b. No.

    c. I do not use this selling technique.

106. "Glad you're doing well, let's discuss your needs." is a transitional phrase that typically:

    a. Moves the seller from the greeting to the warm-up step.

    b. Moves the seller from the warm-up to the qualification step.

    c. Moves the seller from the qualification to the presentation step.

107. "Now that I know your needs, let's look at the product." is a transitional phrase that typically:

    a. Moves the seller from the greeting to the warm-up step.

    b. Moves the seller from the warm-up to the qualification step.

    c. Moves the seller from the qualification to the presentation.

108. "Hello. How are you? Is this your office?" is a transitional phrase that typically:

    a. Moves the seller from the greeting to the warm-up step.

    b. Moves the seller from the warm-up to the qualification step.

    c. Moves the seller from the qualification to the presentation step.

109. "Well, that's our presentation—let's look at your options." is a transitional phrase that typically:

    a. Moves the seller from the qualification to the presentation step.

    b. Moves the seller from the qualification to the close.

    c. Moves the seller from the presentation to the close.

110. "Now that I know your needs, let's set a delivery date." is a transitional phrase that typically:

    a. Moves the seller from the warm-up to the qualification.

    b. Moves the seller from the qualification to the close.

    c. Moves the seller from the qualification to the presentation.

Scoring
Cornerstones of Selling Study
Part IV—Transitional
Phrases and Stressing the Difference
Legend:

TP   Transitional Phrases.

STD   Stressing the Difference.

Instructions:

From the previous *Exercise*, circle the same letters below, including the score. After completing this section, proceed to the *Score Box*. Make certain your answers reflect the way you actually interact with your prospects and customers.

---

91. Stressing the difference means emphasizing the differences between:

    a.   0

    b.   10   STD

    c.   0

92. My purpose in using the stressing the difference process is to:

    a.   0

    b.   10   STD

    c.   0

93. I point out the differences between my employer, products and services and the competition's employer, products and services:

    a.   10   STD

    b.   5   STD

    c.   0

94. My prospects would rate my ability to implement the stressing the difference process:

    a.   10   STD

    b.   5   STD

    c.   0

95. I know what stressing the difference phrases appeal or are acceptable to my prospects:

    a.   10   STD

    b.   0

    c.   0

96. I am most likely to use stressing the difference when:

    a.   0

    b.   10   STD

    c.   0

97. When I do stress the differences between my employer, products and services, and the competition's employer, products and services:

    a.   5   STD

    b.   10   STD

    c.   0

98. I can cite the differences between my employer, products and services and the competition's employer, products and services easily:

    a.   10   STD

    b.   0

    c.   0

99. Which phrase is an example of a stressing the difference statement?

    a.   10   STD

    b.   0

    c.   0

100. Which phrase is an example of a stressing the difference statement?

    a.   0

    b.   0

    c.   10   STD

101. A transitional phrase is a phrase that helps a seller to:

    a.   10   STD

    b.   0

    c.   0

102. An effective use of a transitional phrase:
    a.   5   STD
    b.   5   STD
    c.   10   STD

103. I know what transitional phrase's are effective for my selling style:
    a.   10   STD
    b.   0
    c.   0

104. My prospect would rate my ability to move smoothly from idea to idea as:
    a.   10   STD
    b.   5   STD
    c.   0

105. I can use a variety of transitional phrase's comfortably and whenever I desire:
    a.   10   STD
    b.   0
    c.   0

106. "Glad you're doing well, let's discuss your needs" is a transitional phrase that typically:
    a.   0
    b.   10   STD
    c.   0

107. "Now that I know your needs, let's look at the product." is a transitional phrase that typically:
    a.   0
    b.   0
    c.   10   STD

108. "Hello. How are you? Is this your office?" is a transitional phrase that typically:

    a.   10   STD

    b.   0

    c.   0

109. "Well, that's our presentation—let's look at your options." is a transitional phrase that typically:

    a.   0

    b.   0

    c.   10   STD

110. "Now that I know your needs, let's set a delivery date." is a transitional phrase that typically:

    a.   0

    b.   10   STD

    c.   0

Score Box
Cornerstones of Selling Study
Part IV—Transitional
Phrases and Stressing the Difference
Instructions:

Total your score for each category and place it on the line to the right of the appropriate classification:

	Subelement	Total Points
STD	— Stressing the Difference	_____
TP	— Transitional Phrases	_____

Find your scores for each category (STD, TP) on the following page. If your total score for any category is 80, 70, or 60, read both phrases (just above and below that score). The following analysis is based on the accuracy of your selections. It reviews only the technical aspects of your selling practices.

If your responses are correct and a reflection of your actual selling performance, the following assessment will be accurate. Other critical factors that impact your selling success (for example: appearance, body language, confidence, voice, product or service knowledge, and subelements of the sale) are not factored into this study.

Awareness Level and Probable Tendencies
Cornerstones of Selling Study
Part IV — Transitional Phrases and
Stressing the Difference

STD	TP
80 – 100 Points	
You can easily point out the differences between yourself and the competition in a positive way. Your abilities in this area give you great advantages over other sellers.	You possess a solid understanding of the use of transitional phrases. You should be able to select just the right phrases to make smooth transitions from idea to idea.
70 – 80 Points	
When you want to, you point out the differences between yourself and the competition in a positive way. Your skills in this area can be improved with a little more effort.	You have the knowledge to move gracefully and professionally from one step of the sale to the next. With a bit more awareness and practice you will outperform other salespeople.
60 – 70 Points	
Your STD abilities will vary according to your attitude. If you feel comfortable, you will use the STD process well. But negative prospects may undermine your efforts.	When you keep your mind on the selling process and listen, you move from idea to idea well. But when you fail to pay attention, you may fumble about in this area.

If you scored 60 points or lower in any of these categories:

a.   Increase your knowledge of the subelement in question.

b.   Practice using the subelement in front of a mirror or with others.

c.   Video tape your roleplays and allow a qualified person to critique you.

Regardless of how well you scored, review the practices recommended in this chapter. Look for those techniques that can help you, and put them to work as soon as possible.

Stressing the Difference

Stressing the difference is also called the *STD* process. Those sales professionals who use the STD technique can testify to its value. Prospects normally want to know the difference between vendors, products, services, terms, after-sale support policies, guarantees, warranties and other factors that could affect them. Salespeople can increase their selling effectiveness by learning and using this important subelement. Only the most confident salespeople use this particular technique with any level of effectiveness. Many sellers who do use this subelement are too obvious in their efforts.

Definition of STD

Stressing the difference is a technique that enhances the image of the products and services presented by emphasizing the differences between them and the competitor's products and services.

Purpose and Objectives of the STD Process

The purpose of this technique is to help sellers better position themselves with their prospects. The STD objectives are:
- To encourage sellers to present their products and services and position them against their competitions' products and services in a positive fashion.
- To get prospects to focus on the value of the sellers' products and services.

STD Types

- Salespeople can stress the differences between what they offer and what their competition offers in the following areas:
- Price
- Delivery
- Reputation
- Availability
- Product quality
- Service quality

- Customer support
- Innovation and creativity
- State-of-the-art technology
- Sensitivity to customer needs and desires
- Willingness to fulfill customer needs and desires

How to Initiate the STP Process

Initiating this technique is best handled by salespeople who understand the importance of the STD process and implement it in a casual and subtle fashion.

Initiating the STD Process in Business-to-Business Sales or Consumer Sales
• "Your present suppliers are charging you 10 percent more than we will. Buy from us and pocket the difference."
• "The other company guarantees its services for three months while we will guarantee your purchase for a year. The difference is significant and the extra coverage may end up saving you a great deal of money."
• "The other group is a fine company. As you probably know, its technicians are new to this business. All of our technicians have been servicing customers like you for over five years. Who would you rather service your equipment?"
• "Most vendors offer their clients an 8-hour customer service line to call in requests and questions. A call to their staff from this area would cost you a long distance charge. And some of the service calls are lengthy. Our customer assistance program offers you an 800 line that is open 24 hours a day

Initiating the STD Process

STD techniques are most effective when:
- Salespeople feel that the differences between their offerings and those of their competition need to be discussed.

- Prospects indicate that they do not understand the differences between the seller's features and benefits and those available from others.
- Salespeople feel that pointing out the differences between their offerings and those of their competitors will strengthen their selling advantages.

The Anatomy of the Sale
Table 5-1
Initiating the STD Process During the Five Steps of the Sale

Legend:

Excellent step to initiate _√√√_
Good step to initiate _√√_
Fair step to initiate _√_
Poor step to initiate_ _

The Five Steps of the Sale	Where To Initiate STD
1. Greeting	1. _ _
2. Warm-up	2. _ _
3. Qualification	3. _√√_
4. Presentation	4. _√√√_
5. Close	5. _√_

STP Pitfalls, Causes and Options

Here is an example of a pitfall sellers can encounter in stressing the differences.

Pitfall—A common STD pitfall occurs when salespeople do not prequalify their prospect's attitudes toward the features and benefits being compared. The prospects will feel that their needs are not going to be met because the sellers are insensitive to their interests and challenges. This pitfall is easily avoided by sellers who thoroughly qualify their prospects before beginning the STD process.

Using Transitional Phrases

There is much to be said about the implementation and use of transitional phrases. The salesperson who masters transitional techniques will discover that prospects will view him as an individual who is:

- Organized.
- Professional.
- Accomplished in the art of communicating with others.

Sellers' abilities to communicate easily and freely are critical to their success. Mastering the use of *transitional phrases* is therefore extremely important to a seller. Although a number of sales reps seem to be spontaneous in the way they introduce transitional phrases, most rely on a series of well-rehearsed phrases and make each sound fresh and off-the-cuff.

Definition of Transitional Phrases

Transitional phrases are statements that help the seller move smoothly from one thought, step, or segment of the sale, to another.

Purposes and Objectives of Using Transitional Phrases

The purpose of transitional phrases is to help salespeople develop continuity and easy movement from one thought to another throughout the selling process. Sellers' objectives in using this discipline are:

- To change the direction of their conversations.
- To allow the sellers the opportunity to demonstrate their thought organization, professionalism and preparedness.

Types of Transitional Phrases

There are many types of transitional phrases. This section focuses on five different categories that allow the seller to move comfortably from the:

1. Greeting to the warm-up.

2. Warm-up to the qualification.

3. Qualification to the presentation.

4. Qualification to the close.

5. Presentation to the close.

How to Use Transitional Phrases

Implementing transitional phrases smoothly can be difficult for salespeople who:

- Are not comfortable with their prospects.
- Do not know exactly what they want to say next.
- Are not well-versed and confident in their selling abilities.

The prospect's personality also comes into play, since the more flexible the prospect, the simpler and faster the transitional process moves. Less flexible prospects will demand more time and effort as the seller moves from one thought to another.

The transitional process can sometimes be aided by the repetition of a certain word or phrase in order to connect different ideas. Different situations call for different transitional techniques. Here are several examples of how to use transitional phrases:

Initiating
Transitional Phrases
in Business-to-Business or Consumer Sales

1. **Greeting to the warm-up**—This is the easiest place to initiate a transitional phrase. Here is an example of a salesperson using a transitional phrase to move from the greeting to the warm-up by calling attention to a trophy in the prospect's office or home:

   Seller: "I noticed the golfing trophy on your credenza. Are you a golfer?"

   From this point, the salesperson can conduct a natural conversation with the prospect regarding the prospect's interest in golf.

Continued on next page.

Initiating
Transitional Phrases
in Business-to-Business or Consumer Sales

2. **Warm-up to the qualification**—This transition can be challenging, even difficult, if the prospect is enjoying the warm-up stage and does not want to discuss business. A seller who makes a rapid change too abruptly during this stage can confuse and sometimes offend the prospect. The salesperson must be careful in leading the prospect from the warm-up to the qualification. This next example demonstrates how to use a transitional phrase to bridge the warm-up and the qualification steps:

    Seller: "Perhaps we should move on, knowing that we might run out of time to discuss some of the business items that may be of greatest importance to you. So please, if I may ask, what are your equipment or service needs in . . ." (the seller then asks the first qualification question).

    Such a transition is usually well received by the prospect and allows both parties to proceed into the qualification without either one feeling rebuffed or confused.

3. **Qualification to the presentation**—This transition can be difficult for sellers who have not positioned themselves well. Difficult as this effort might seem, a few well-chosen words can make it easy:

    Seller: "With the information we've just reviewed, the following will answer your needs."

    Following this statement the salesperson should proceed into the presentation.

4. **Qualification to the close**—This kind of transition demands that the salesperson be courageous enough to trial close without making a presentation. Critical factors that a seller has to remember about the qualification-to-close transition are:

    a. The seller must advantageously position the close.
    b. The seller has to select a closing style that is suitable to the prospect's personality.

    Continued on next page.

Initiating
Transitional Phrases
in Business-to-Business or Consumer Sales

c. The seller must time the close for a moment in which the prospect is receptive to making a decision.

A transitional phrase is rarely needed between the qualification or the presentation and the close. Such a statement can delay and even hamper the closing process. If too much is said between these two steps, the buyer may get the impression that the sales rep does not want to make the sale. Since making the transition from the qualification to the close is similar to making the transition from the presentation to the close, see the transition examples in the next step, (5) Presentation to the close.

5. **Presentation to the close**—This is a transitional process that is much easier to implement than most people realize. For example:

Seller: "That completes the presentation. Now _____." (A closing statement is made at this point.)

or

Seller: "Thank you for your interest in our products and services. _____" (A closing statement is made at this point.)

Note that both examples are very short. Again, the seller does not want a wordy transitional phrase to get in the way of the closing process.

Initiating Transitional Phrases

The time to use a transitional phrase is:
- When the seller wants to move from one thought to another.
- When it is appropriate to move from one stage of the sale to the next.
- When the seller wants to change the focus of a discussion and can use a transitional phrase to lead the listener.

The Anatomy of the Sale
Table 5-2
Initiating Transitional Phrases During the Five Steps of the Sale

Legend:

Excellent step to initiate _√√√_
Good step to initiate _√√_
Fair step to initiate _√_
Poor step to initiate_ _

The Five Steps of the Sale	Where To Initiate Transitional Phrases
1. Greeting	1. _√√√_
2. Warm-up	2. _√√√_
3. Qualification	3. _√√√_
4. Presentation	4. _√√_
5. Close	5. _ _

Transitional Pitfalls, Causes and Options

Here are some examples of pitfalls that may be encountered by a salesperson using transitional phrases.

Pitfall #1—The lack of transitional phrases (rushing from thought to thought without the formal use of the transitional process) can confuse prospects and cause them to question the seller's competency. The transition is too abrupt when the seller or prospect cuts the transitional process short. In either case, one of the parties is attempting to rush the selling process.

In viewing thousands of actual selling situations, my associates and I have discovered that many salespeople do not listen to themselves or to their prospects carefully enough. In debriefing sessions after these sales calls (and away from their prospects) these same sellers were rarely aware that:

- They had rushed the selling process.
- The prospect had rushed the selling process.

- Their thoughts had been poorly developed or tied together.

It is essential that salespeople be well-versed in the application of transitional phrases, and discipline themselves to complete their thoughts by carefully bridging the various parts of the sale. Abruptness and rushing the sale can be easily avoided if the sellers are confident, capable and empathize with their prospects' situations and needs. They must listen conscientiously to what they are saying to their prospects, and to what their prospects are saying to them.

Pitfall #2—Lack of forethought in the selling process results in a disjointed presentation. Here sellers are not thinking ahead and preparing themselves to handle the process right. Successful sellers:

- Think the selling process through beforehand.
- Take into consideration the variables involved.
- Plan their selling approach using previous information.

Pitfall #3—Lack of practice in making a smooth transition from thought to thought creates a jumbled and disorganized presentation. A good number of salespeople overlook the fact that successful sellers have to do their homework. They neglect to evaluate their selling situations beforehand, riding on the hope that things will automatically and easily fall into place during the sale. Before even entering a sale, the salesperson should plan his or her selling approach and tactics, including appropriate transitions.

What to Do After the Sale Has Been Successfully Completed

Once a transaction is completed a salesperson should avoid *buying back the order*. Buying back the order happens when the seller talks too much after the close and says something that causes the prospect to back out of the transaction. Once the transaction is complete, the salesperson should avoid issues that would cause the customer to have second thoughts about the purchase.

The Importance of
Developing a Positive Sales Presentation

Every veteran seller understands the value of developing a positive flow—creating a positive communication process with the prospect. The easiest way to develop a positive flow is by:

- Offering the prospect several options.

- Discussing issues that are of interest to the prospect.

- Remaining positive even if the prospect is in a negative mood.

Positive salespeople solve more of their prospect's problems and make more sales than sellers who allow negative prospects to affect their attitudes and selling styles. Salespeople who lack confidence tend to become negative and defensive and lose sales as a result.

Each element of a sale is a process unto itself with its own set of objectives, rules and possible pitfalls. The salesperson who studies and masters each step can then go on to master other selling processes, such as negotiations. It takes time, effort and smart work to improve one's selling style. However, once the mastery of the basics is complete, the seller usually realizes that all the time, effort and smart work are essential to his or her selling success.

Chapter Summary

1. *Stressing the difference (STD)* enhances the image of what is being presented by emphasizing the differences between your products and services and the competitor's products and services.

2. *STD* is important to both you and your prospects because prospects normally want to know the difference between vendors, products, services, terms, after-sale support policies, guarantees, warranties and other factors that could possibly affect them.

3. *STD* objectives are:
   - To get the prospect to focus on the value of your products and services.
   - To assist you in positioning the value of your products and services against those of your competitor in a positive fashion.

4. You should employ *STD* techniques when:
   - You feel these differences need to be discussed further.
   - You feel these differences will strengthen your position.
   - The prospect does not understand the difference between your products and services and those available from others.

5. *Transitional phrases* (TP's) are statements that help you move from one thought, step or segment of the sale to another.

6. This chapter focused on five different categories of *transitional phrases* that allow you to move comfortably from one step of the sale to the following step:
   - Greeting to the warm-up
   - Warm-up to the qualification
   - Qualification to the presentation
   - Qualification to the close
   - Presentation to the close

7. The time for you to use a transitional phrase is:
   - When you want to move from one thought to another.
   - When it is appropriate to move from one stage of the sale to the next.
   - When you want to change the focus of a discussion and can use a transitional phrase to lead the listener.

8. *Buying back the order* is a phrase that refers to a situation in which the seller who talks too much after the close and says something that causes the customer to back out of the transaction. Once you complete your transaction, avoid issues that would cause the buyer to have second thoughts about his or her purchase.

9. It is easy to develop a positive flow with the prospect by:
    - Offering the buyer several options.
    - Discussing issues that are of interest to the prospect.
    - Remaining positive even if the prospect is in a negative mood.

10. Nobody wants to be sold to. Nobody wants to be sold at. Yet most people are willing to discuss the details.

11. Your selling efforts will become easier in time with practice, and if you repeat the following statement vigorously, silently, and humbly just before you call on your prospects and customers: "The sale is complete. I am here merely to reach an agreement about the details."

The Next Step

Read, study, practice, review
and analyze everything you come into
contact with regarding communications and sales.
Do this again and again and again until all of this
information becomes a natural part of your
selling and communicating style.

Anyone can make an easy sale. However, there are few easy sales to be made. That is one reason why so few salespeople truly succeed at their profession. Another reason why few succeed is a lack of awareness of the basics of their profession.

The 10 Cornerstones of Selling offers you the opportunity to master some of the subtle nuances of your profession. As you have already discovered, some of these techniques are simple and easy to use while others are far more challenging.

Regardless of how you feel about any of these techniques, I suggest you learn and practice each skill. Be prepared for the sale that may demand the extra effort that a particular technique may offer you.

I have never met a salesperson who failed because of overpreparation. But I have met many through meetings, seminars, and conventions who were dissatisfied with their performance because they were not prepared with the product knowledge and selling skills necessary to do their jobs in a professional fashion.

May you fill your customer's needs and prosper in every positive way your mind and heart desire.

Glossary

A

Action

Fourth of the four elements of a sale in which the seller attempts to close the prospect. See also *AIDA*.

Advantage

An advantage is what the feature will do for its user. See also *Benefit, Cornerstones of Selling, FAB, Feature*.

AIDA

The four elements of a sale. AIDA outlines what the seller must accomplish during the face-to-face sale. AIDA is an acronym for:

A: *Attention*—the stage in which the seller captures the prospect's attention.

I : *Interest*—the stage in which the seller develops the prospect's interest.

D: *Desire*—the stage in which the seller builds prospect's desire.

A: *Action*—the stage in which the seller gets the action (commitment) desired of the prospect.

The theoretical flow of the selling process. A technique also used in all forms of advertising (radio, television, billboard, direct mail, print), public relations and public speaking. One of eight major areas that sales managers use to assess a salesperson's abilities. See also *Action, Anatomy of the Sale, Attention, Desire, Interest*.

Anatomy of the Sale

An overview of the dynamics of the selling process and how they relate to each other. For example:

Four Elements		Five Steps	
What sellers want from their customers or prospects		*How sellers go about achieving their objectives*	
1. Attention	>	1. Greeting	
1. Attention and	>	2. Warmup	
2. Interest			
2. Interest	>	3. Qualification	
3. Desire	>	4. Presentation	
4. Action	>	5. Close	

See also *Action, AIDA, Attention, Desire, Five Steps of the Sale, Interest.*

Attention

First of the four elements of the sale in which the salesperson attempts to capture the buyer's attention by discussing issues that are of interest to that person. See also *AIDA.*

B

Basic Steps of the Sale

See also *Five Steps of the Sale.*

Benefit

A benefit is the end reward or profit that a user will derive from the original feature. A benefit is usually expressed as a profit or savings in time, money, effort, safety or security. For example, the copier seller could extend the FAB process by saying, "This savings of time will save you and your organization money as well!" See also *Advantage, Cornerstones of Selling, FAB, Feature.*

Buying Signal

Any indication by prospects that they are ready to buy. See also *Cornerstones of Selling.*

C

Close

A point of agreement. Step of the sale in which the salesperson finalizes an agreement (close) with the buyer. For example, agreeing to:

- A future appointment.
- Actual purchase of a product or service.
- Disbursement of monies owed the vendor.
- Allowing seller to make a presentation or demonstration.
- Allowing seller to gather data vital to the sales presentation.
- Meeting with the decision maker or purchasing committee or other interested parties.
- Consideration as a vendor or alternate vendor (placement on the approved vendor's list).
- Selling and buying terms—size, price, color, flavor, quality, quantity, delivery day, financing option.
- Agreement dealing with some other service or product-related issue.
- Extending the salesperson special privileges other than those mentioned thus far.

The close is the fifth and final step of the sales transaction. A close is also a negotiating ploy. It is one of eight major areas that sales managers use to assess a salesperson's abilities. Depending upon its use, this tactic can be classified as a low or high-risk negotiating technique. See also *Anatomy of the Sale*.

Cornerstones of Selling

Sales practices that support the Five Steps of the Sale:

1. Presenting Features, Advantages and Benefits
2. Using the WIIFM Technique
3. Recognizing Buying Signals
4. Asking the Right Questions
5. Handling Objections
6. Placing the Customer in the Picture of Success

7. Pairing

8. Romancing the Sale

9. Stessing the Difference

10. Using Transitional Phrases

See also *Advantages, Benefits, Buying Signals, FAB, Features, Pairing, Placing the Customer in the Picture of Success, Romancing the Sale, Stressing the Difference, Transitional Phrases, WIIFM.*

D

Desire

A wish or nonessential want. That which a person or group may want but does not need. One of ten factors that motivate a buyer to make a purchase. The third element of the selling process called AIDA in which the seller tries to entice the buyer into making a purchase. See also *AIDA*.

F

FAB

FAB is the act of explaining to prospects what advantages and benefits they (their organizations or families) derive from features. See also *Advantage, Benefit, Cornerstones of Selling, Feature.*

Feature

A feature is a statement regarding the salesperson's product, service or organization. See also *Advantage, Benefit, Cornerstones of Selling, FAB.*

Five Steps of the Sale

A logical approach to verbal sales communications. The five steps consist of the:

1. Greeting

2. Warm-up

3. Qualification

4. Presentation

5. Close

See also *Anatomy of the Sale, Close, Greeting, Presentation, Warm-up, Qualification*.

Four Elements of the Sale

Theoretical foundation upon which the selling process is built. What the seller wants to accomplish. See also *AIDA*.

G

Greeting

The first step of a sale in which the salesperson meets the buyer and introduces himself or herself; the step which sets the tone for the transaction. See also *Anatomy of the Sale, Five Steps of the Sale*.

I

Interest

The second element of the selling process called AIDA in which the salesperson stimulates the buyer's interest in the vendor's presentation, goods and services. See also *AIDA*.

P

Pairing

The act of allying the vendor's reputation, the quality of a product, service, guarantees, warranties, price, customer support programs, delivery time or other business conduct to that of another successful organization that the customer holds in high regard. See also *Cornerstones of Selling*.

Placing the Customer in the Picture of Success

A technique in which the seller helps the customer visualize and mentally or emotionally experience the benefits he or she will derive from using the product or service. See also *Cornerstones of Selling, Romancing the Sale*.

Presentation

The fourth step of the sale; the demonstration or discussion of a product or service during which the salesperson gives the buyer enough data to make a positive buying decision. Also used in reference to:

- One's appearance.
- The appearance of a product or brochure.
- The entire time a seller spends with a prospect.

See also *Anatomy of the Sale, Five Steps of the Sale*.

Problem Solver

A person who tries to:

- Fill the prospect's needs.
- Meet the prospect's challenges.
- Answer the customer's problems.

See also *Problem Solving*.

Problem Solving

The art of reaching a solution or conclusion to some need, challenge or problem. See also *Problem Solver*.

Qualification

The practice of determining another's needs or position by asking questions or offering probing statements. The third step of the sale in which the salesperson asks questions (known as the Six W's) to determine the listener's legitimacy as a prospect. See also *Anatomy of the Sale, Five Steps of the Sale, Six W's*.

R

Romancing the Sale

Making the product or service or the customer's use of it appear positive. Romancing the sale is similar to the technique of placing the customer in the picture of success. See also *Cornerstones of Selling, Placing the Customer in the Picture of Success.*

S

Sales

A function of marketing. A form of communicating with others. The amount sold (normally expressed in financial terms or in units). The act of bartering and negotiating products or services for something of value.

Salesperson

One who negotiates and barters products, services or money for something of value. Also referred to as: Account Executive, Account Manager, Account Representative, Agent, Canvasser, Clerk, Counterjumper, Counter Person, Door Knocker, Door-To-Door Salesperson, Drummer, Field Person, Field Rep, Field Salesperson, Hawker, Huckster, Inside Rep, Inside Salesperson, National Account Manager, National Account Salesperson, Peddler, Sales Consultant, Sales Engineer, Salesgirl, Saleslady, Salesman, Sales Rep, Saleswoman, Seller, Selling Agent, Shopgirl, Shopman, Solicitor, Traveling Salesman, Vendor. See also *Sales.*

Selling Steps

See *Five Steps of a Sale.*

Six W's

Six types of questions a salesperson must ask a buyer during the qualification stage of a sale. The gathering of information the seller needs to tailor his or her presentation to the buyer's needs. Questions that encourage customers to reveal their needs and agenda. The Six W's are:

- Who
- What
- Where
- When
- Why
- HoW

See also *Qualification*.

Steps of the Sale

See *Five Steps of a Sale*.

Stressing the Difference

A technique that enhances the image of the products and services presented by emphasizing the differences between them and the competitor's products and services. See also *Cornerstones of Selling*.

T

Transitional Phrases

Statements that help the seller move from one thought, step or segment of the sale to another. See also *Cornerstones of Selling*.

Trial Close

A subtle approach testing a prospect's readiness to buy.

W

Warm-up

The second step in the sales process in which the seller's objectives are to:

- Encourage the buyer to relax.
- Become accustomed to the environment.
- Establish a rapport with the buyer by discussing issues of interest to that person.

Casual conversation dealing with topics the buyer:

- Relates with.
- Enjoys talking about.
- Feels are nonthreatening.
- Responds to in a positive fashion.

See also *Anatomy of the Sale, Five Steps of the Sale.*

WIIFM

An acronym for the prospect's or customer's question, "What's in it for me?" In other words, how will the customer profit by purchasing the seller's products or services? See also *Cornerstones of Selling.*

Index

A

B

Benefits, 31, 34, 37

Buying signals, 43-48
    recognizing, 43
    definition of a, 43
    purposes and objectives of a, 43
    types of, 43-44
    how to evaluate and respond to or test a, 44
    initiating a, response in business-to-business or consumer sales, 45
    when to respond to a, 45
    when, occur during the five steps of the sale, [*see* the anatomy of the
    sale, table 2-3]
    pitfalls, causes and options, 46-48

C

Cornerstones of selling study,
    part I, buying signals, what's in it for me, and features, advantages and
    benefits, 30
    part II, asking questions and handling objections, 66
    part III, pairing, romancing the sale, and placing the customer in the
    picture of success, 106
    part IV, transitional phrases and stressing the difference, 137

Cornerstones of selling, the,
    identifying, 4-5
    subelements, 4
    the importance of understanding, 8-10

Close, 5-6
    [*see* anatomy of the sale (table 1-1)

F

G

H

I

N

O

P

Q

S

Stressing the difference, 137-140
awareness level and probable tendencies, 137
definition of, 138
how to initiate, process, 139
initiating process, 139-140
initiating the, in business-to-business or consumer sales, 139
pitfalls, causes and options, 140
purpose and objectives of, process, 138
types, 138-139
[*see* also the anatomy of the sale, table 5-1]

T

Transitional phrases, 137-144
awareness level and probable tendencies, 137
definition of, 141
how to use, 142
initiating, 144
initiating the, in business-to-business or consumer sales, 142, 144
pitfalls, causes and options, 145-146
purpose and objective of, 141
types of, 141-142
using, 141

W

Warm-Up
anatomy of the sale (table 1-1), 5-6

Lizardy Associates Live Seminars —

Programs That Will Make a Positive
Difference for You and Your Organization

The person who conducts your training session or addresses your regional and national conferences is critical to your program's success. That is why you should call us before planning your next business event. Our staff of professionals is well-experienced in a variety of subjects for short speaking engagements and longer training sessions:

Sales

- Telemarketing
- Sales Planning
- Time Management
- Customer Sensitivity
- Developing a Proposal

- How to Close
- Sales Psychology
- Handling Objections
- Territory Management
- Selling to a Committee

- Sales Auditing
- Sales Negotiations
- Retail Selling Skills
- Improving Your Image
- Business-Business Selling

Marketing

- New Markets
- Marketing Auditing

- Image Making
- Marketing Planning

- Strategic Planning
- Understanding the Market

Customer Contact

- Telephone Skills
- Customer Psychology

- HRD C.C. Skills
- Selling Skills for C.C.

- Technical C.C. Skills
- Handling Difficult People

Professional Skills

- Planning Skills
- Dealing With Change

- Stress Management
- Communication Skills

- Platform Techniques
- Negotiating Techniques

Supervisory and Management Skills

- Selection
- Motivating
- Strategic Planning
- Supervisory Training

- Recruiting
- Interviewing
- Time Management
- Management Training

- Delegating
- Train the Trainer
- Leadership Training
- Management Negotiations

For more about our consulting services, speakers, trainers, subjects and course offerings, write or telephone for a free Lizardy Associates Capabilities Review:

**Lizardy Associates • P.O. Box 270468 • San Diego, CA •
92198
Tel. 619-485-0929**